Public Engagement Made Easy

Local leaders don't need to become professional facilitators or hire expensive consultants to run a great meeting. *Public Engagement Made Easy* offers practical and affordable methods that bring ease to one of the most challenging aspects of any local leader's role: involving the public. The tools and techniques in this book will empower planners, public managers, decision-makers, and other leaders to implement effective public engagement programs that build trust within communities and contribute to successful decisions that stand the test of time.

Susan Charland, AICP, is a city planner, facilitator, and public engagement specialist. She has dedicated her career to helping local government leaders successfully engage with their communities. Charland provides training sessions on engagement techniques and has spoken about the topic at conferences around the US.

SUSAN CHARLAND

Public Engagement Made Easy

A Guide for Planners and Policymakers

Routledge
Taylor & Francis Group

LONDON AND NEW YORK

Designed cover image: Lily Coleman-Bondgren

First published 2025
by Routledge
4 Park Square, Milton Park, Abingdon, Oxon, OX14 4RN

and by Routledge
605 Third Avenue, New York, NY 10158

Routledge is an imprint of the Taylor & Francis Group, an informa business

British Library Cataloguing-in-Publication Data
A catalogue record for this book is available from the British Library

Library of Congress Cataloging-in-Publication Data
Names: Charland, Susan, author.
Title: Public engagement made easy: a guide for planners
and policymakers / Susan Charland.
Description: New York, NY: Routledge, 2024. |
Includes bibliographical references and index. |
Identifiers: LCCN 2023059115 (print) | LCCN 2023059116 (ebook) |
ISBN 9781032587141 (hardback) | ISBN 9781032583884 (paperback) |
ISBN 9781003451174 (ebook)
Subjects: LCSH: Participation. | Public speaking. | Decision making. |
Communities—Social aspects. | Leadership.
Classification: LCC HM771 .C43 2024 (print) | LCC HM771 (ebook) |
DDC 302/.14—dc23/eng/20240223
LC record available at https://lccn.loc.gov/2023059115
LC ebook record available at https://lccn.loc.gov/2023059116

ISBN: 978-1-032-5-8714-1 (hbk)
ISBN: 978-1-032-5-8388-4 (pbk)
ISBN: 978-1-003-4-5117-4 (ebk)

DOI: 10.4324/9781003451174

Typeset in Joanna MT
by codeMantra

Contents

Figures

I was motivated to write this book by the hundreds of practitioners, authors, researchers, and public officials who perform public service in their day-to-day work. This book is the result of years spent working alongside these people, and I'm grateful for having the chance to learn from them. This book would not have been possible without the help of an amazing community of friends and colleagues.

A huge thank you goes to Joe Bovenzi, Ben Wrobel, Matt Leighninger, and Christopher Dunne for providing thoughtful, thorough, and incisive feedback on my initial drafts.

For their willingness to talk with me and share their professional experience, feedback, and advice—about both public engagement and writing—I want to thank Tina Nabatchi, Matt Roland, Carol & Terry Lewis, Sean Maguire, David Rouse, and Ian Coyle.

I am grateful to my husband, Kurt Charland, for his constant support and encouragement throughout the writing process. I also want to thank my family and friends who were instrumental in cheering me on: Andrea Hopkins, Ruth & Roger Hopkins, Judy Shone, Emily Sanders Hopkins, Karen LaFauci, Sherry Rettew, and Anne Redmond Jen Topa.

A special thanks to Lily Coleman-Bondgren for creating the beautiful cover art.

Thanks to the editorial team at Routledge; Megha Patel, Selena Hostetler, and Kathryn Schell. Thank you for your kindness and enthusiasm in walking me through the publishing process.

Artificial intelligence disclaimer

None of the text in this book was developed using artificial intelligence large language models (LLMs). Nor was any grammar, presentation, or organization assisted by artificial intelligence. I did not use any prompts to generate content or use of LLMs as a "writing partner" to modify or otherwise edit text that I had written.

I realize that in a few years (or months), my reluctance to use LLMs to assist in writing this book may seem quaint. AI is predicted to grow increasingly ubiquitous in technology and our day-to-day lives. My objections to using LLMs in this specific context may be resolved in the coming months and years. But for better or worse, this book is 100% human-powered.

My concerns about AI-powered LLMs in 2023 stem from: (1) their lack of attribution in their output and (2) how the models are built and trained. It is unclear whether original content entered into a LLM chat box will be used for future training and machine learning (although I suspect it will). LLMs were allegedly trained by scraping original content from across the internet. A portion of the content in this book was inspired by my personal blog about public engagement, which I authored and maintained for three years, between 2020 and 2021. I learned in July 2023 that my blog content was likely scraped at least two years prior for LLM training. (Chat GPT-4, developed and owned by OpenAI, completed its first training in 2021, although the exact parameters of the training are not public information.) This means the content I posted on my blog may have been incorporated into these models and may be used without attribution.

One

PLANNING IS PUBLIC ENGAGEMENT

I never set out to have a career in public engagement. My dream was to design cities. As a high school student, I read *The Geography of Nowhere* and became convinced that society's problems could be fixed if only we could design better cities. I knew that I wanted to help improve people's lives and strengthen our communities by improving the built environment. I devoured books on city planning. I evangelized to my friends. I made ironic holiday cards with pictures of vacant shopping malls. As co-editor of my college magazine, I convinced the other editors to raid our tiny printing budget to pay an honorarium for my high school hero, James Howard Kunstler, to fly to Ohio and speak to our student body. I wanted to spread the message. After college, I went to work in the planning department of a small city in Colorado. Then on to get a master's degree, internships, and finally a "real job." All this time, the thought never crossed my mind that I could or would have a career in public engagement.

Being an urban planner was different than what I envisioned it would be. I wasn't me sitting in a sunny office dreaming up perfect plans for perfect neighborhoods and cities, and then handing those plans down to the grateful masses. No. That's not what happened. I learned that planning is not that simple or glamorous. It can be muddled and frustrating. It's process-y and bureaucratic—and it's often highly political. It's hard work, often tedious, with long hours, and seemingly endless night meetings. The day-to-day work is stressful and fast paced. And yet, projects take years—entire careers—to materialize. The pace of community change is slow and it can sometimes feel like time is going backwards.

Twenty years into my career, I am yet to create a plan in a room by myself. I am yet to present a plan to a community and be showered with gratitude and admiration, or watch a community diligently implement

DOI: 10.4324/9781003451174-1

everything in "my" plan. Instead, I have worked on bits and pieces of plans, and written and researched and attended meetings for years to achieve seemingly tiny wins. I have seen projects start, stop, and die. I've watched implementation happen in small increments, never knowing if the existence of a plan had made any difference at all. Being a planner didn't look anything like what I thought it would.

Planning isn't really about the plans at all. Although I've seen tremendous changes in communities I have lived and worked in, from Portland, Oregon to Detroit, Michigan to small towns in Upstate New York, the role I played in these transformations was miniscule. And that's what planning is all about. It's not about the pieces of paper, maps, or documents. It's not about any one person. Planning is the act of people working together in groups to solve problems and create plans.

Planning is an activity that people do together by participating. The real achievement of planning is in the collaboration, dialogue, and compromise. And fundamentally, it's about communities and people participating in decisions that affect their lives. Public engagement isn't just one aspect of planning. Public engagement is planning.

The problem with public engagement is that no one wants to do it
Despite its central importance to the field of city planning (and policymaking in general), I have observed over the years that the number one challenge with public engagement is that no one really wants to do it. I'm not talking about corrupt or authoritarian leaders (although those people certainly don't want to do it). I'm talking about planners, policymakers, and decision-makers like you and me, who have dedicated our careers to public service and creating a better quality of life for communities across the US. People who believe as wholeheartedly as I do that engaging community members in decisions that affect their lives is one of the most important features of our democracy.

Even the true believers don't really want to do it
We know we should do it. But many policymakers approach the public with reluctance. Maybe we acquiesce to minimum regulatory requirements or find ourselves selling an idea to the public rather than asking for ideas. In other cases, we stonewall and ignore the public altogether. There is often a significant gap between what we think is right and our ability to practice it.

Many of us have been led to believe public engagement is difficult, expensive, and even dangerous. Maybe you've been told it's something for the "people person" in your organization. Or that it's best to just leave it alone. Maybe you had a bad experience at a public meeting and now you dread the prospect of facing an unreasonable crowd. Maybe you believe the public isn't qualified to have an opinion. Maybe you fear losing control of a decision process. Given all the objections and fears (and let's face it, things often do go wrong), it's understandable why no one *really* wants to do it.

It's not just planners who don't want to do public engagement. The public often doesn't want to do it, either. But for different reasons. They're busy people with jobs and kids. They don't have an extra two hours in the evening to attend a public meeting. Or maybe they have learned through lived experience that their feedback won't matter, anyway. They feel participating will be a waste of their time.

Why public engagement is like eating vegetables

For years, I have compared the work I do to parents trying to convince toddlers to eat their vegetables. It was only while researching this book that I was reminded where I learned that comparison. It was Sherry Arnstein's 1969 article *A Ladder of Citizen Participation*, where she originally compared public engagement to eating spinach, noting that "no one is against it in principle because it is good for you."[1] The principle is easy. It's in the practice of doing something good for us that is hard.

Public engagement has a reputation of being a messy, amorphous activity and has a way of highlighting some of society's most uncomfortable tendencies: fear, pain, denial, revenge, tribal loyalty, and greed. Exposing our work to the public's harsh opinions, unpredictable emotions, and potential bad behavior can strike terror in even the most seasoned professional. We would prefer not to be that vulnerable. Likewise, asking planners and decision-makers to be happy about seeking the opinion of hostile strangers is like putting a plate of spinach in front of a toddler. We predict there will be a big mess to clean up afterwards.

Yet many of you reading this book joined the profession with a sense of public duty and have, if not a solid determination, then at least a vague sense that involving the public in local government decisions is good. Maybe you have a general sense of justice. Maybe you want to believe we, as planners and public policy officials, are helping to uphold ideals of freedom and democracy. Maybe you're not into ideals, but you're aware of the practical benefits of involving the public, such greater support and legitimacy of public decisions.

But here is the paradox: While the *thought* of engaging the public can elicit fear and discomfort, the *act* of engaging the public can bring out the best in us. Helping members of a community participate in important public decisions that impact their lives, and the lives of their children, can be one of the most gratifying aspects of being a planner or policymaker.

The importance of public engagement in local decisions
The ability to do public engagement well, particularly at the local level, is an overlooked aspect of our democracy. At the same time, public engagement in local decisions has become increasingly necessary, particularly in recent years. Local governments, agencies, and non-profits have a unique opportunity to strengthen our democracy by involving community members in a meaningful way. Public engagement can help us rebuild some of the bonds that have been broken over the past few years. But it will only work if planners and local leaders commit to integrating quality public engagement into their decisions.

Quality public engagement helps resolve conflict, heal divisions, build trust among citizens, and build accountability. When local leaders engage the public to identify critical issues early in a decision process and bring multiple perspectives to the table, those leaders actively build buy-in for local decisions. Likewise, decision-makers who implement better public engagement will be more effective and successful. As humans, we have an innate desire to participate in decisions that affect us. That desire is also the root of our democracy, of government of the people, by the people, and for the people. The process of making decisions together not only makes our government better, but it also fosters connections between us and brings meaning to our lives.

I come to the field of public engagement not just as a planner and a consultant, but as someone interested in how and why humans gather and connect—and how and why people decide things as groups. Group participation and collective decision-making has been fundamental to our experience as humans since the dawn of our species. Likewise, in our modern democracy, the ability to assemble and meet is considered fundamental to our rights in the US.

For the last decade, I have worked with policymakers, planners, technical experts, and decision-makers of all kinds to improve their public engagement processes. But my journey to this place has not been smooth or linear. It has been fraught with experimentation and failure.

While practicing public engagement as a consultant, I have authored a blog about my public engagement experiences. I have spoken about it at conferences. I have designed and led trainings on public engagement for elected officials, planners, and students. I have been fortunate to have the opportunity to hear from hundreds of people who do the day-to-day work of engaging the public. Through those experiences, I have learned what many decision-makers consider to be the most challenging pain points, what scares them the most, and what successful public engagement looks like.

But I have also struggled. I've had a chance to reflect on my mistakes—and I share many of those mistakes with you in this book. In his book *Four Thousand Weeks: Time Management for Mortals*, Oliver Burkeman calls upon the wisdom of Richard Bach, who famously said, "You teach best what you most need to learn." I believe the same is true of authors: we write the book we most need. I spent years struggling with public engagement, trying to understand how it fits in the bigger picture of governance and democracy, why we should do it, and why so many of us are reluctant to do it. I have yet to reach perfection in the public engagement realm. And like Oliver Burkeman, I admit that I wrote this book for myself as much as I did for you.

I believe everyone can conduct public engagement well. You don't need to be an expert facilitator. You don't need to be the mayor of a big city. You don't even need to be the boss. And fortunately for all of us, good public engagement does not rely on one's ability to stand on a stage and sell a crowd on the merits of a public decision or project. Good public engagement simply requires intention, humility, and authentic curiosity about the humans in our midst.

Is this book for you?

Maybe you've picked up this book because you don't like public meetings, but you're obligated to hold them. Maybe your aim is to acquire skills in managing unruly crowds, handling difficult people, and dealing with grandstanding. Or perhaps you are a policymaker who is enthusiastic about leading community discussions, and you want to learn more about involving community members in crucial public decisions.

You are in the right place.

Whether you instinctively shy away from public engagement, find yourself on the fence, or wholeheartedly embrace it, my aim with this book is to equip you with tools that will transform both your perception and practice of public engagement.

This book is not just for planners. It is for **anyone involved in decision-making** within an organization, whether that is a government agency, a quasi-governmental organization, a non-profit, or a neighborhood organization. Although my experience is centered on local government decisions, public engagement is simply about opportunities to involve people who are interested in and affected by a decision, whether that is decision made by a government, a non-profit organization, or a private sector company. The concepts and tools presented in this book can be adapted to fit your context, whatever that may be.

This book is for the **people responsible for carrying out public engagement**, whether you are a planner, a decision-maker, or staff at a public agency. It is solidly grounded in the realities of day-to-day practice of policymaking and with the awareness that we all have first-hand experiences with the complexity of political power in the US, at all levels of government. It is meant to be thought-provoking, encouraging, and instructive for policymakers who work at all levels of government, but especially local government. This book is meant to help you start improving your public engagement efforts now. Not after you "10x" your budget or hire a team of 20 engagement specialists. You don't have to wait until we have fixed the structural inequities of US democracy and our capitalist economic system. This book provides a way to think about public engagement in practical terms as well as the tools and techniques that I have found useful throughout my career.

HOW THIS BOOK IS ORGANIZED

In writing this book, I have two goals, which I present to you in two parts.

1. To persuade you of the need for better public engagement.
2. Share concrete steps and techniques I have learned over my career that I believe will help you design and implement effective public engagement practices and programs.

The first part of this book describes the problem. I hope to convince you, reader, of the perils of bad public engagement and the benefits of good engagement. The second part of this book communicates practical steps you can take to make public participation easier for you and your organization.

I designed this book for maximum flexibility, both in terms of the order you decide to read something and how much time you want to devote. I usually pick up a book, scan the table of contents, pick through a few sections that sound interesting, and depending on what I find in those sections, I may return to the beginning chapters. I wrote this book to allow a reader to drop in anywhere. You can read this book in linear fashion or use the table of contents as your map to find the sections that most appeal to your interests and goals. You can also use the index to find topics of interest.

TERMINOLOGY

The terminology we use to describe the activities and players involved in public decisions is constantly evolving and it is possible that by the time you read this book, there may be new terms in play, and old terms that are no longer considered appropriate or inclusive. The title of this book uses the term "public engagement." But I know there is a wide variety of terms used by practitioners across the US. The term public engagement is simply my preferred way to describe *what we do*. My colleagues and partners also use other terms, such as public participation, civic engagement, stakeholder engagement, citizen participation, deliberative democracy, participatory governance, co-governance, and others. I recognize that there are settings in which each of these terms carries a specific definition. Many practitioners use these terms interchangeably and that most fall under the umbrella of participatory democracy.

This book describes the people *who initiate* public engagement in a variety of ways, too. These terms include planners, policymakers, decision-makers, sponsors, convenors, practitioners, and facilitators. Finally, I use different kinds of words to describe the people *who participate* in public engagement. These terms include the public, community members, advocates, participants, and interested/impacted parties. I don't intend to confuse readers with this, but I prefer not to restrict the discussion to one single moniker within each category. I find it helpful to use these terms in specific contexts where necessary to help communicate the nuances of leadership and different power dynamics that exist.

I find it helpful to think about the people involved in the decision process in terms of three types.

Decision-makers. The first bucket is the decision-maker, whether that is an individual, a committee, an agency, or staff. These may include the following terms:

- Elected officials
- Appointed officials
- Administrative staff
- Convenors
- Sponsors

The public. The second bucket is the public, for which I alternate between "public," "interested parties," "community members," and "participants." In some specific cases, I may use the term "residents" or "neighbors" to describe the public, but I acknowledge those can be exclusionary terms in the context of certain public decisions because they may not signal inclusion of all types of impacted parties, such as business owners, members of adjacent communities, undocumented people, New Americans, and people who are unhoused. Terms for the general public may include:

- Community members
- Participants
- Residents
- Neighbors
- Advocates
- Interested/impacted parties

Public engagement professionals. The third type of people involved in public engagement includes public engagement professionals. These are people who design, implement, and/or facilitate participatory activities. These people are sometimes called facilitators, public engagement specialists, deliberative practitioners, mediators, and facilitative leaders. They may be staff within a government agency, consultants, or volunteers.

- Planners
- Public managers
- Facilitators
- Staff

Many planners play the role of a public engagement professional at some point in their careers. If you have any doubt about whether you are a public engagement professional, remember this: If you are planning any kind of public meeting on behalf of a decision-maker, you are a public engagement professional.

A FOCUS ON LOCAL GOVERNMENT

The scale of impact and opportunity for public engagement in local government decisions cannot be overstated. According to the Census of Governments, there were 90,088 state and local government entities in the US in 2022.[2] Local government leaders, such as mayors, town board members, and county executives (and many others), govern almost the entire population of the US. Local governments employ about 14 million people. This means there are literally millions of people in the US who are directly involved in the daily administration of our government, creating, and implementing policy, and making local public decisions that directly impact our lives.

Research shows that Americans trust their local governments more than other levels of government. The Pew Research Center, based in Washington DC, has been exploring levels of public trust in the US government at all levels since the 1950s. According to Pew, public trust in the federal government peaked in 1964, when 77 percent of the population said they "trust government to do what is right just about always/ most of the time." The percentage of people who now say that has since declined to about 16 percent as of 2023.[3] By contrast, trust in local and state government appears to be higher. About 66 percent of Americans say they have a "favorable view of their local government" compared to just 32 percent who have a favorable view of the federal government. Similarly, a 2021 Gallup Governance poll concluded that almost 70 percent of the population said they trust local governments to handle local problems.[4]

Perhaps one reason Americans trust their local governments more is that the workings of local government decisions are typically less partisan than other levels of government. While trust in federal and state governments tends to be divided along partisan lines (with the party in power engendering the most trust from the corresponding party), Democrats and Republicans have similar levels of trust in their local governments, with 73 percent of Democrats and 70 percent of Republicans reporting a "great deal" or "fair amount" of trust in local government.[4]

In addition to engendering more trust, local governments can have a more immediate and direct impact on people's lives than state and federal governments, by virtue of what local governments do: public safety, land use regulation, long-range planning, sanitation, open space preservation, fire protection, economic development, education, and many others. Local officials make decisions about a wide variety of issues, such as building new playgrounds, upgrading a sewer treatment plant, or purchasing new snowplows. Local government leaders across America make thousands of decisions every day that have a direct impact on the public.

The impacts go both ways. Local government is also considered more accessible to the public than state or federal government. Some scholars consider local government the most "permeable" and "proximate" level of government.[5] In the 1830s, Alexis de Tocqueville made a similar observation about local governments, stating in the case of townships that "law and government are closer to those governed." Indeed, local governments are typically run and staffed by people in the community, including business owners, neighbors, and advocates. Members of the general public are more likely to be personally connected to a representative of their local government than state or federal government. For these reasons, this book focuses primarily on local government decisions.

* * * * * *

The ideas presented in this book are not meant to be a definitive solution, but rather a small contribution to a larger dialogue. Like all things in planning and public engagement we are in constant conversation with ourselves and our communities about what our work means and why we do it. Much like learning to eat our vegetables helps us become healthier people, I hope the knowledge and practical guidance in this book will empower you to make positive improvements to how you, as a practitioner, engage the public throughout your career.

REFERENCES

[1] Arnstein, S., A Ladder of Citizen Participation. *Journal of the American Planning Association*, 1969. **35**(4): pp. 216–224.

[2] Bureau, U.C., *Survey of Public Employment & Payroll Summary Report: 2022*, P.V. Nicholas Saxon, Sean Wilburn, Sarah Andersen, Dylan Maloney, and Ross Jacobson, Editor. 2023, U.S. Census Bureau.

[3] Center, P.R., *Public Trust in Government 1958–2023*, Pew Research Center, Washington, D.C. 2023.

[4] Brenan, M., Americans' Trust in Government Remains Low, in *Gallup*. 2021, Gallup.

[5] Nabatchi, T. and L.B. Amsler, Direct Public Engagement in Local Government. *American Review of Public Administration*, 2014. **44**(4_suppl): pp. 63S–88S.

Part One

INTRODUCTION

In the military, law enforcement, and professional car racing, the term "going sideways" describes an otherwise linear operation that unexpectedly suffers a catastrophic breakdown and devolves into chaos. Like many things that go sideways, my first disastrous public meeting caught me completely by surprise. I was fresh-faced in my career as an urban planner, and my boss had given me the chance to organize and host my first public meeting. (As a consulting planner, my job was to organize all aspects of the public meeting on behalf of a local municipality. This included the design of the meeting, invitations, promotion, facilitation, and follow-up.) After two months of planning, the night of the public meeting finally arrived. I got to the middle school cafeteria early, wearing my best suit—and feeling totally overprepared. After arranging the chairs and tables, setting up the screen and projector, and organizing cookies and coffee, I excitedly stationed myself at the entrance to welcome everyone. I wondered who would show up and what they would have to say. In planning for this meeting, I had followed the rules, checked the boxes, and done what those before me had done. I hadn't given much thought to what would happen *after* we opened the doors at 6:00 pm. But as a line formed at the sign-in table and the public drifted into the auditorium, my anxious attempts to welcome people were met with cold stares, long sighs, and frustrated grumbling. Within minutes, I could tell something was off. I couldn't connect with people. I could feel my skin go hot and my stomach tighten. I started to sweat. This was not what I expected.

This crowd was angry

Members of this community had come to "my" meeting to express their outrage about a public decision I had invited them to discuss. As

DOI: 10.4324/9781003451174-3

we convened the meeting, I watched participants settle into their seats; middle aged couples in jeans, a nurse in scrubs and clogs, a few retirees adjusting their hearing aids, a man sporting a "Ray's Electric" t-shirt. But most of them were wearing a deep frown, slumped into the rows of folding chairs, with their arms crossed.

I could *feel* that this meeting was not going to go well.

And, no, this story does not have a happy ending.

The meeting did not go well. It turned out the people who came to this meeting were upset about a lot of things. As I convened the meeting and thanked everyone for coming, I could see my clients, representatives of the local municipality, huddled in the back of the room, looking concerned. I had practiced my presentation at least eight times and was very proud of all the information I had ready to share. But before I could even flip to my first PowerPoint slide, a man in the back of the room raised his hand and asked, "Why is this the first time I'm hearing about this project?" As I stumbled over an answer about the public hearing process, another member of the audience called out that she, too, had not heard anything about this project until the day before and had only found out because her next-door neighbor mentioned it in passing. A few others in the audience nodded and agreed aloud. Five more hands went up. One man said no one had asked him what he thought about the project, to which almost everyone in the room agreed. And then the barrage began in earnest. I stood at the front of the room as members of the audience launched complaints at me like tennis balls, one after another. I could barely return one before the next came hurtling toward me.

This is a terrible project.

How could you think the community would want this?

You don't care what we think anyway.

This is a waste of taxpayer dollars.

Some things never change.

Our opinion doesn't matter to you.

This is a done deal!

Other comments took the form of personal insults directed at me. For being the stranger at the front of the room. For wearing a suit. For not having real answers. For nervously trying to calm the room. Members of the community were upset and many were on the verge of outrage.

In the face of these intense emotions, it's easy to blame participants for being unreasonable, or to blame their political leanings, demographics, or a host of other factors. But those factors did not matter. The truth is, it didn't matter what kind of project it was, nor did the politics of the attendees. Those details were not what caused the public's outrage.

What caused the public's outrage was badly executed public engagement.

Disastrous community meetings are so common and so familiar to the American public that we can't resist making them the subject of humorous commentary. Think of how the TV show *Parks and Recreation*, which features a chipper bureaucrat named Leslie Knope claiming that angry meeting participants are simply "caring loudly," could become one of the most popular TV shows of its era.[1]

As Priya Parker observed in her 2018 book *The Art of Gathering: How and Why We Meet and Why it Matters*, "much of the time we spend in gatherings with others disappoints us."[2] There are many reasons our gatherings are so disappointing. We lack purpose. We're bad at logistics. We run away from difficult topics. While Parker's book focuses on dinner parties and business conferences, the sentiment captures perfectly how most of us feel about public meetings. It is no surprise that many of us would prefer to avoid public meetings at all costs rather than face the potential of being disappointed, whether it's due to boredom, anger, or despair.

A public meeting-gone-sideways is not just an uncomfortable moment for the person facilitating the meeting. There are many costs of doing public engagement badly, from lost time and money to damaged trust. The disastrous public meeting I recount above was not just a failure and embarrassment for me professionally but also damaging to the community. Public outcry eventually scuttled the project, but only after months of protests and legal appeals. I had wasted my client's time and money and possibly damaged the community's trust.

That night I made a promise to myself that such a failure would never happen again. It was a grand promise that I fully intended to keep. But I didn't. I didn't know how. For a few years after that meeting, I repeated that same scenario more times than I care to admit. I reached a point where I believed horrible public meetings were just part of the job. I believed it was the reality of being a city planner. Eventually, I turned these feelings outwards and my colleagues and I began to blame the "unreasonable public" for the way these meetings went. And at my lowest point, I wondered if it would be easier if no one showed up at my meetings.

The act of designing and implementing public engagement can be an emotional journey for public managers. That journey starts when we contemplate engaging the public. At first, there is uncertainty and then fear. It can quickly descend to panic and retreat. Left unchecked, this journey can continue downward, producing damaging tendencies such as secrecy, resistance, blame, stonewalling, and even authoritarianism.

But there is another direction this journey can go, where our fear can be transformed into courage and purpose. This journey started for me on the night of that first public meeting-gone-sideways. It led me on a challenging path of intense learning and self-reflection, with some success mixed in.

What I have learned in the last two decades is that the factors contributing to the meeting being a failure began long before we opened the doors at 6:00 pm. My team and I could have changed the atmosphere and the outcome of that meeting if I had known then what I know now.

The balance of this book shares what I have learned in the last two decades of doing public engagement, sometimes badly and sometimes successfully. I hope that these lessons can help make public engagement easier and more effective for everyday planners and policymakers like you.

REFERENCES

[1] TV show. *Parks and Recreation*. Season 1, Episode 2. NBC. 2009.
[2] Parker, Parker, *The Art of Gathering: How We Meet and Why It Matters*. 2018. Penguin Publishing Group New York: Riverhead Books.

Three

INTRODUCTION

Everyone has the right to be involved in decisions that affect their life.
International Association of Public Participation (IAP2)

Have you ever asked yourself, *"What does public engagement mean to me?"* If not, I invite you to do it now. At first glance, this may appear to be an easy question to answer. You might say public engagement is when we get input or seek feedback from the public. Some may say public engagement is when community members provide comments at a public hearing. Or perhaps you might say public engagement is what happens when a government body seeks the involvement of those who are interested in and/or will be impacted by a decision. And all of these would be true.

But what makes an activity public engagement versus something else entirely? As planners and policymakers, many of us would recognize certain activities to be public engagement: a town hall meeting, a charette, or a public workshop. But we may be less clear about *why*. What makes those activities public engagement and not something else? What about attending a protest, filling out an online survey, lobbying, or voting? Would those activities be considered public engagement? We know there are many ways to be involved in policy decisions and the workings of larger society. But not all forms of involvement are the same. The way we define public engagement impacts the way we design and implement it, whether we achieve our objectives, and how successful we are.

The American Institute of Certified Planners (AICP) Code of Ethics and Professional Conduct says that, "our primary obligation as planners and active participants in the planning process is to serve the public interest." Serving the public interest can take many forms, such as paying attention to how decisions are interrelated, understanding the long-term consequences of our work, exploring our own biases, and incorporating

DOI: 10.4324/9781003451174-4

equity principles as a foundation to planning work. Serving the public interest can also mean that we "facilitate the exchange of ideas and ensure that people have the opportunity for meaningful, timely, and informed participation in the development of plans and programs that may affect them."[1]

In that sense, public engagement is a core principle of responsible planning and a primary way to serve the public interest.

In practice, public engagement is about more than an exchange of ideas and participation—**it is about sharing power** (and the ways in which decision-makers do that—or don't). The way we define public engagement can either obscure that truth or help us address it head on. Given that local decisions have a major impact on the lives of almost everyone in the US, the way that we define public engagement isn't just a means to help us in our own practice. How we define public engagement will impact the way local leaders make thousands of decisions that affect millions of Americans every year. When it comes to understanding public engagement and doing it well, the stakes are high. The way we define public engagement impacts the role we play in supporting our democracy every day.

WHAT PUBLIC ENGAGEMENT IS NOT

Before we dive into some of the most useful definitions, it is helpful to understand public engagement relative to what it is not. In my practice, I use three questions to help me differentiate public engagement from other types of civic involvement: Who is doing the asking? Who has the power to make the decision? How much power is being shared? The answers to these questions will tell us if the activity we're embarking on is public engagement or something else. When there is a mismatch between who is doing the asking and who has the power to decide, the activity is probably not public engagement.

To explore this concept further, let's look at an example of a situation that can be easily mistaken for public engagement. When a grass-roots neighborhood organization convenes a public meeting to seek input about a government decision, there is a mismatch between who is doing the asking (in this case, the neighborhood organization) and who is making the decision (the local government). If the decision-maker isn't doing the asking, then it's less likely that power will be shared. And in that case, it's not public engagement. The grass-roots organization may be doing advocacy, lobbying, or public relations. All three of those activities have an important role in democratic society. But they are not public engagement. On the other hand, if the government (the decision-maker) convenes the public to ask for input about a government decision, it's more likely that power can be shared. **A key defining element of public engagement is whether the entity with the power to decide is doing the asking—and sharing influence over the decision.**

In this chapter, we will explore these concepts in more detail, review widely accepted definitions of public engagement, and look at how public engagement is shaped by political power and influence.

Many of us find definitions, organizing principles, and frameworks to be abstract and theoretical; i.e. not helpful in the day-to-day work of making policy decisions. But these same definitions and organizing principles have the power to make your practice easier. Such a foundation creates a starting point where you can then apply and adapt the principles to your specific circumstances, such as the type of entity you represent, the capacity of your organization, the complexity of your project, and the expectations of your community.

DEFINITIONS OF PUBLIC ENGAGEMENT EVERY PRACTITIONER SHOULD KNOW

While I encourage every practitioner to read widely on the topic of participatory democracy and public engagement, I understand this isn't practical for everyone. Since the title of this book is *Public Engagement Made Easy*, I have attempted to make this part as easy as possible for you to read. The following paragraphs summarize some of the most relevant and practical definitions and frameworks I have found, which have helped me the most throughout my career, and that I believe can best help you in your day-to-day work.

Like many forms of participatory democracy, public engagement exists in an elusive space. Americans are not used to talking about nuanced layers of democratic participation. Participatory democracy is sometimes referred to as "democracy beyond elections" because it describes a form governing in which community members do more than just vote for representatives; they participate directly in the decisions that affect their lives. At the same time, participatory democracy doesn't mean the public gets to vote on every government issue and policy. In that way, participatory democracy is not purely direct democracy, nor is it purely representative democracy. Rather, it exists in a space somewhere between the two.

For many Americans, voting for their representatives is the extent of their participation. Direct democracy, however, is when the people rule themselves by making laws and decisions without elected intermediaries. Direct democracy in its purest form would involve the people voting on all laws, bills, and court decisions. In theory, direct democracy ensures the greatest amount of transparency and accountability because decisions are made publicly and the ultimate responsibility for success or failure is placed on the people, rather than the government. But examples of direct democracy are typically limited to local and state governments in the form of ballot initiatives, referendums, and recall elections—all situations where the public votes directly on a decision.

There aren't many real-world examples of direct democracy because it is challenging to implement when there are large groups of people involved. Imagine if everyone in the US were expected to vote on every law and policy. We could spend 100 percent of our days debating and voting on laws. Would we be able to make decisions or get anything done? Probably not. So instead, we practice representative democracy by electing people to United States Congress, state legislatures, and local government bodies.

But Americans are not always satisfied with a system in which people vote once every few years and hand over decision-making power to the people they elect. Sure, the public may agree with elected officials on certain issues. But the fact that people support an elected official's ten-point platform does not mean people trust their elected officials to know how the public feels about all issues and decisions. So, while most Americans understand it's more efficient to elect representatives to make decisions for us, most of us still want to have some influence over those decisions. Participatory democracy provides that middle ground. It is a process that community members across the US can use to influence decisions even though they aren't making those decisions directly.

When you consider the difference between purely representative democracy and fully direct democracy, you start to see that these two concepts vary greatly in the amount of influence the public has over everyday policy decisions. Participatory democracy simply means the public has influence over decisions that affect their lives. But if the public's influence goes beyond voting for representatives and stops short of voting for everything else, what does it look like? How much influence does the public have? And how does the public express that influence?

The following sections describe some of the most accepted definitions of public engagement. These definitions represent various ways of thinking about (and doing) public engagement. Some of these definitions portray public engagement in a linear way (Ladder of Citizen Participation), while others define engagement in terms of categories and choices (Spectrum of Public Participation). Still others define public engagement in terms of methods (Thick, Thin, Conventional). I have worked with all these definitions at one time or another, using them standalone, or by selecting pieces of each that fit into the context of my work. At the end of this chapter, I describe a framework for public engagement that I have developed over the course of my career by combining elements of these definitions with my own experience and the needs of the communities with which I have worked.

Public engagement on a ladder, a continuum, and a spectrum

Our modern understanding of public engagement in the US can be traced back to 1969, to a policy analyst named Sherry Arnstein, who was working as a special assistant in the U.S. Department of Health, Education, and Welfare (later called the Department of Health and Human Services). Arnstein felt motivated to address what she saw as a failure of government officials to adequately implement citizen participation. In her pivotal article for the *Journal of the American Planning Association* entitled "A Ladder of Citizen Participation," she critiqued the way powerholders conducted public participation, calling it an "empty ritual," and declaring that "participation without redistribution of power is an empty and frustrating process for the powerless."[2]

Arnstein described the dominant approach to participation in the 1960s as insincere at best (and in her words, a "sham") writing that while no one seemed to be against the principle of this important "cornerstone of democracy," real-life enthusiasm for its practice waned when it was advocated for the "have-nots." The entire discussion around participation, she wrote, was "exacerbated by rhetoric and misleading euphemisms."[2]

The ladder itself describes degrees of citizen participation, organized into eight rungs, ranging from nonparticipation, to tokenism, to citizen power. The steps on the ladder include *manipulation* (rubber stamp form of nonparticipation), *therapy* (where the powerless are pathologized and asked to change their attitudes), *informing* (a one-way flow of information with no channels for feedback or negotiation), *consultation* (inviting opinions and feedback from the public), *placation* (cherry-picking a few "worthy" members of a community to participate on a board or committee), *partnership* (power is redistributed via negotiation between the public and decision-makers), *delegated power* (where the public has dominant decision-making authority or veto-power), and *citizen control* (where members of the public fully govern a program or institution without intermediaries).[2]

Even today, I hear members of the public use terms such as "manipulated" and "placated" to describe how they feel treated when participating in a local government decision. At the same time, many members of the public understand, on some level, the various forces involved in creating that sense of powerlessness. Local government decision processes tend to exist toward the bottom of the ladder simply because they are designed to rely heavily on minimum legal requirements and bureaucratic public hearing procedures. Planners and local leaders are often encouraged to follow established legal procedures, which require only the bare minimum of engagement. Planners can face an uphill battle when trying to convince decision-makers to move up the ladder into forms of engagement that share influence and power. (Chapter 9 describes how legal minimum requirements for public engagement can often create an environment of frustration and mistrust.)

It is hard to overstate the significance of Arnstein's ladder in the planning field. The "Ladder of Citizen Participation" has been cited or cross-referenced over 17,000 times in academic journals, books, and other resources.[3] That doesn't even include the hundreds (or even thousands) of online citations and references in blogs, articles, presentations, and student papers. The article has influenced multiple generations of planners and public policy professionals across disciplines. Virtually all planners are exposed to the ladder at some point in their educational journey. The longevity of the ladder is due to its enduring relevance: it is as relevant today as it was in 1969.

Some criticisms of the ladder argue out that Arnstein was clearly admonishing anything that falls on the lower rungs of the ladder. And some practitioners maintain that some elements of the lower rungs, such as "informing" can be legitimate activities and important aspects of any public engagement program. Arnstein herself acknowledged that public engagement in the real-world is far more complex than anything captured in the ladder, but that the ladder's simplicity is what makes it so useful. Indeed, the ladder continues to be one of the most ubiquitous and recognizable concepts in the planning field today.

Following Arnstein's breakthrough article, the 1970s and 1980s brought about an era of exploration of participation in the planning world, where practitioners began to define participation "not as a single act, but a scale of possibilities."[4] Researchers and theorists developed a variety of participatory and "communicative" models for planning. By the 1990s, planners had begun to rally around ideas of deliberative, discursive models of participation that emphasized inclusive dialogue, learning, and group problem-solving.[5]

In later decades, theorists adapted and built upon Arnstein's ladder. John Clayton Thomas, author of numerous scholarly articles and the book *Public Participation in Public Decisions* developed a model for participation based on five approaches (autonomous managerial decision, modified autonomous managerial decision, segmented public consultation, unitary public consultation, public decision).[6,7] Thomas wrote that each approach to decision-making is suited to different kinds of participation techniques. For instance, public decisions that will be decided by a manager without any public engagement require different kinds of techniques than decisions for which a manager will seek feedback from the public before deciding. This, in turn, requires different techniques than a manager who shares the problem with the public and reaches a solution collaboratively with the community.

Another influential framework for public engagement was first published in 1996 by the Organization for Economic Co-operation and Development as part of a volume called Responsive Government: Service Quality Initiatives. The authors described a "continuum" of participation in policy decisions, from "minimum participation" to "maximum participation." Along this continuum are five types of public engagement: information, consultation, partnership, delegation, and control. The authors say these five types are not meant to be steps. Instead, they represent a "set of choices for public officials."[4] Selecting the appropriate choice on the continuum depends on the goals of the people involved (both the decision-maker and the public). Authors Bishop and Davis further built upon the concept of a continuum by modifying the categories, including one category called "standing," where third parties could become involved in the decision through legal means, such as courts, tribunals, and other statutory processes.[4]

The Ladder of Citizen Participation and variations of participation continuums are important antecedents to what many consider the most recognizable framework for public engagement in modern times: the International Association of Public Participation (IAP2) Spectrum of Public Participation.

IAP2 is a leading international organization focused on advancing the practice of public participation, which it defines as an activity that "involves the public in problem-solving or decision-making and uses public input to make sustainable decisions."[8] While the Spectrum of Public Participation may be the most widely cited element of their framework, the organization offers two other complementary pillars, including Core Values and a Code of Ethics. These pillars, including the Spectrum of Public Participation, were developed to help decision-makers and practitioners define the public's role in a decision-making process. Based on decades of research, IAP2's Spectrum of Public Participation includes five categories of participation, from "inform" on the left to "empower" on the right. The spectrum is structured such that the categories toward the right of the spectrum represent a higher degree of influence over a decision process than the categories to the left of the spectrum.

The Spectrum of Public Participation is not intended to be a litmus test or a series of sequential steps to be followed during a decision process, where we start on the left and finish on the right. Rather the spectrum presents different categories or levels of participation that can be selected by practitioners based on the specific context of the decision at hand. Many practitioners will point out that being on the right end

IAP2 Spectrum of Public Participation

IAP2's Spectrum of Public Participation was designed to assist with the selection of the level of participation that defines the public's role in any public participation process. The Spectrum is used internationally, and it is found in public participation plans around the world.

INCREASING IMPACT ON THE DECISION

	INFORM	CONSULT	INVOLVE	COLLABORATE	EMPOWER
PUBLIC PARTICIPATION GOAL	To provide the public with balanced and objective information to assist them in understanding the problem, alternatives, opportunities and/or solutions.	To obtain public feedback on analysis, alternatives and/or decisions.	To work directly with the public throughout the process to ensure that public concerns and aspirations are consistently understood and considered.	To partner with the public in each aspect of the decision including the development of alternatives and the identification of the preferred solution.	To place final decision making in the hands of the public.
PROMISE TO THE PUBLIC	We will keep you informed.	We will keep you informed, listen to and acknowledge concerns and aspirations, and provide feedback on how public input influenced the decision.	We will work with you to ensure that your concerns and aspirations are directly reflected in the alternatives developed and provide feedback on how public input influenced the decision.	We will look to you for advice and innovation in formulating solutions and incorporate your advice and recommendations into the decisions to the maximum extent possible.	We will implement what you decide.

© IAP2 International Federation 2018. All rights reserved. 20181112_v1

Figure 3.1 IAP2 Spectrum of Public Participation.

of the spectrum (empower) does not necessarily equate to "better." And many public engagement processes will work within multiple categories. Depending on the stage of the decision process, practitioners may choose to jump around, employing different levels of public engagement at different stages of the decision process.

While the spectrum is not meant to be a series of steps, a decision process most certainly *is* a series of steps. Any rational decision process used by decision-makers should follow a series of sequential steps, from project inception to the development of options, all the way to the decision itself. Later chapters of this book describe how best to align public engagement with a linear decision-making process. For now, it's enough to know that the IAP2 Spectrum can be enormously helpful to you in the context of an overall decision process when used to determine which level of participation is most appropriate for each step in the decision process.

Public Engagement as "thick," "thin," and "conventional"

Two leaders in the field of public engagement, Tina Nabatchi and Matt Leighninger, have been researching and publishing on the topic of public engagement for well over a decade. Nabatchi is a Professor of Public Administration and International Affairs at the Maxwell School of Citizenship & Public Affairs at Syracuse University. Leighninger is the Director of the Center for Democracy Innovation at the National Civic League. Together, they authored *Public Participation for 21st Century Democracy*, in which they acknowledge the challenge of defining public engagement but offer a fitting description of the field as one where "people's concerns, needs, interests, and values are incorporated into decisions and actions on public matters and issues."[9]

In *Public Participation for 21st Century Democracy*, Nabatchi and Leighninger further define participation as three main types: (1) thick, (2) thin, and (3) conventional. **Thick participation** can be thought of as the most intensely focused, "time-consuming" form of participation.[9] A key characteristic of "thick" participation is that it often takes place in small groups and provides an opportunity for participants to deliberate, in depth and share detailed perspectives and ideas. According to the authors, the best kinds of thick participation not only involve small group discussion, but also leverage existing networks to attract participants, and involve an intentional form of group discussion that allows participants to establish trust, develop goals, frame the issues, and define actions. Examples of thick participation include gatherings such as design charettes, participatory budgeting, and the World Café technique.[1] They are considered thick because all three techniques include in-depth, detailed discussions and group problem-solving.

By contrast, **thin participation** describes a sort of light touch approach that is designed to engage large numbers of individuals, rather than people in groups. It is a less overall effort and expenditure of brain power for participants and is usually a smaller time-commitment. Thin participation does not require participants to immerse themselves into the background and technical details of a project, nor does it require a back-and-forth dialogue with other participants. Think of short online surveys, pop-up booths, and open house meetings where participants can drop in anytime throughout the evening.[9]

The authors point out that there are strengths and weaknesses of both thick and thin forms of participation. As with any form of public engagement, the relative success of any method or technique relies on how it is implemented—and importantly, whether it is a one-off activity or part of a cohesive and focused public engagement program. Thin participation techniques might not be effective in every context because they do not allow in-depth discussion and sharing of information. Thick participation can be expensive and time consuming to organize, making it much more likely that convenors will not be able to sustain thick activities throughout an entire decision process, or replicate them with parallel decisions. These shortcomings are aptly summarized as, "thick engagement doesn't scale and thin engagement doesn't stick."[9]

But not all types of public engagement have pros and cons. Some just have cons. This leads us to the third type of participation, which the authors describe as "conventional." In their analysis, **conventional participation** is the most common form of participation. It is also considered the least effective. Unfortunately, conventional participation is what most planners, decision-makers, and members of the public experience most often. Think of public hearings, planning board meetings, and town hall-style meetings. This kind of involvement is typically the result of regulation (federal, state, or local requirements to hold public hearings) and is usually organized around bureaucratic rules of order (such as public notice requirements as well as strict rules and time limits for spoken testimony). Such practices are not generally well-liked among members of the public because they are not transparent, nor do they engender trust among the public.

Not surprisingly, conventional participation is considered problematic and potentially harmful to the public because it erodes public trust and creates a sense of powerlessness.[9] My experience over the last decade would support this conclusion. Although conventional participation processes were originally designed to provide an opportunity for the public to have a voice and to ensure transparency and accountability in government decisions, few of us could make a case that it does any of those things. The mismatch between the stated aims of conventional participation and the reality creates a cognitive dissonance, not only for participants, but also for organizers.

Consider this example of conventional participation in real life: Members of a community receive an invitation to a public hearing where decision-makers will decide whether to approve or deny a proposal to construct a bike lane on Main Street. The invitation says, "We want your input!" Some community members are inspired to attend the public hearing to provide their input. Some are in favor of the bike lane. Others would like to ask questions and suggest minor changes to the design. Others are opposed to the bike lane. When these community members arrive at the public hearing, they find out there is no opportunity to ask questions or engage in any conversation with decision-makers. They may become frustrated, and even enraged to discover they must wait three hours to provide their input—and even then, they will be limited to two-minutes (two minutes?!). To compound the frustration, they may also find out that no one is required to respond to their comments, and so no one does. After they speak for two minutes, the hearing simply proceeds as if community members are invisible. I have personally witnessed this scenario many times. It happens every day somewhere in the US. It is understandable that this kind of conventional participation and can lead community members to feel disillusioned, powerless, and likely distrustful of government decisions.

PUBLIC ENGAGEMENT IN THE WILD: THE CORE ELEMENTS

You may be asking yourself what all of this means for your day-to-day practice. Let's step back and draw some practical conclusions about how public engagement is defined and what that means for planners' day-to-day work in public engagement. Nabatchi and Leighninger's definitions provide a way to understand public engagement in terms of conventional, thick, and thin activities. Arnstein, IAP2, and others conceptualize public engagement as a ladder, a continuum, and a spectrum.

All these concepts give practitioners a flexible way to plan and implement what is otherwise an overwhelming activity.

Over the last decade of my career, I have selectively incorporated aspects of each of these definitions and frameworks in my work to help me to communicate and implement public engagement programs. I've summarized in the following sections how I have adapted these definitions and frameworks into my practice as five core elements. When put together, these core elements can be an easy way to define whether an activity is public engagement…or something else. The core elements not only explain what public engagement is in simple terms; they contend with the complex relationship between public engagement and political power—and provide a path to address these complexities head on.

The core elements of public engagement are:

1. Public engagement is for public decisions.
2. Public engagement is initiated by decision-makers.
3. Public engagement involves (voluntarily) shared influence.
4. Public engagement strives for consensus.
5. Public engagement builds capacity.

Element #1: Public engagement is for public decisions. There is general agreement in the literature that public engagement is a term reserved for situations where there is a *public* interest or topic at hand. A lesser understood notion is that not only does the participation need to occur in the context of a public topic, but it also specifically needs to be a public decision. In the US, a public decision is generally understood as one that is made by those with political authority to do so, which is a government entity (local, state, or federal) or a quasi-government entity. For the activity to be considered *public* engagement, it must be something that happens in the context of decisions made by such entities.

Element #2: Public engagement is initiated by decision-makers. If public engagement is something that happens only when there is a public decision, then does it matter who is initiating the participation? Yes. Earlier in this chapter I noted the importance of identifying "who is doing the asking." Why does it matter who initiates? The answer to that question reveals an important picture of political power and influence. Activities initiated by the public are not public engagement, but something else entirely, such as community organizing, advocacy, and grass-roots movements. Those are worthy forms of involvement that play an important role in our democracy. But since those activities are not initiated by those with decision-making power, they are not public engagement. Public engagement is initiated by decision-makers (usually governments) and happens when decision-makers invite the public to inform or influence a public decision. In short, public engagement happens when those who hold the power to make a public decision *choose* to talk with the people affected by the decision.

Element #3: Public engagement involves (voluntarily) shared influence. The awkward reality of public engagement, as it is defined in the previous core elements, is that it exists within a hierarchical power dynamic, where decision-makers have the power to choose when to engage, who to engage, and how. Yet, one of the most fundamental aspects of public engagement is that it must involve shared influence. To share influence, decision-makers need to acknowledge their own power role in the overall decision-making process. That is, they have the power to make the final decision. Public engagement happens when those with decision-making power find at least some aspect of the decision that the public can influence. Without shared influence, it's not doing public engagement, but rather, something altogether different, such as public relations, marketing, or education.

The concept of shared influence has far-reaching implications for inclusion and equity as well. As the practice and theory of public engagement has evolved, the importance of equity and inclusion has become evident. Inclusion is an idea that many planners and decision-makers can understand and embrace: it means that we make sure representative cross-section of a community is invited and encouraged to participate, and that a diverse set of perspectives are in the room.

But an inclusive process is not necessarily an equitable one. A process can appear to be equitable because there are many perspectives taking part in the conversation. But if the feedback received from the public during those conversations does not influence the decision, that process isn't really equitable. And, by definition, that process isn't truly public engagement. An equitable process is one that involves the sharing of influence (i.e. power). If there is no opportunity for influence, we're not really doing public engagement. And what we're doing is certainly not equitable.

If shared influence is key to public engagement, can you have equitable outcomes without ceding power to the public? To answer that question, let's take a closer look at the power dynamics inherent in public engagement and how that can affect one's day-today practice. At its most basic level, public engagement can take many forms—but is always grounded in the idea that decision-makers are somehow sharing power with the public. As the authors of *Mapping Public Participation in Policy Choices* aptly say, "Somewhere between policymaking by administrative fiat and direct democracy lies the terrain for participation."[4]

Decision-makers of all kinds, including elected local government officials, are given the political and legal authority to make certain decisions by virtue of being elected and the rules and procedures they are bound to uphold. The public, on the other hand, does not have the legal authority to make those decisions. But that does not mean the public has no power at all. Instead, the public has a different kind of power. It isn't political authority, but rather political *influence*. Political influence refers to the ways people can affect political decision-making in ways other than with legal authority. Political influence is expressed as lobbying, signing a petition, protesting, messaging in the media, and campaigning. Except for voting (either to elect a decision-maker or to make a decision via referendum), the public is generally limited to tools of influence, while decision-makers use tools of legal authority. This is the space into which many planners are squeezed when they plan and implement a public engagement program. In the sandwich of political power, practitioners are the cold cuts folded between two slices: (1) top-town political authority and (2) bottom-up political influence.

We generally think of political authority expressed by decision-makers as "top down," whereas the political influence expressed by the public is "bottom up" (or grassroots). Think of it as top-down authority and bottom-up influence. The paradoxical power dynamic of public engagement and what differentiates it from activism or community organization is that public engagement happens when decision-makers with political authority proactively ask for their own decision-making authority to be influenced by the public. Another way to put it: **public engagement is an activity in which the people in power ask the public to disrupt their own decision authority.**

But this is not the same as self-policing, nor is it a benevolent or altruistic activity. Remember, the public always has *some form* of influence, whether that is achieved via cooperative means (such as lobbying), adversarial means (such as protest), or even violence. There are many practical and politically expedient reasons for public authorities to engage in the seemingly paradoxical activity of public engagement. The benefits of doing this include building public trust, making better decisions, and achieving greater compliance to laws and policies. (see Chapter 6 for more detail on the benefits of public engagement). The practice of public engagement means sharing power. That requires understanding the complex dynamics between political authority (top-down) and political influence (bottom-up) with the goal of making better decisions that improve the lives of the greatest number of people.

Element #4: Public engagement strives for consensus. Even when decision-makers share influence in a decision, that does not always mean they are able to achieve 100 percent agreement among all parties. In many cases, there is ongoing disagreement about a decision, opposition, and even outrage. Even when a good faith effort has been made to address all issues and concerns, there may still be a lack of total agreement. It's usually after my clients have made a real effort to address concerns, only to find that there is still opposition to the decision, that they come to me and ask me how to reach consensus. My response is usually: that depends on how you define consensus.

There is generally a lack of understanding about what consensus really means. And this misunderstanding can impact whether someone is open to consensus-building (to many of my clients, it seems idealistic and complicated), and more importantly, whether consensus can be successfully achieved. Consensus is often confused with other things, such as majority vote or unanimity. While unanimity may be the result of consensus-building process, it is not the same thing. Unanimity refers to complete agreement. Not surprisingly, unanimity is hard to achieve and can be prone to coercion.

Consensus, however, is about finding the "most agreeable decision," within a group, which means finding some form of agreement among most participants while also addressing objections and concerns of the few.[10] After good faith efforts have been made to address the interests of everyone, the result of the consensus-building process is more often a decision that everyone can live with, as opposed to a decision that everyone is jumping for joy to support. The result may be "tacit acceptance" of the decision by those who disagree, or just enough agreement that an agency believes it has legitimacy in making a decision. This tension lies at the heart of public engagement and shared influence. Decision-makers may share influence, but they "reserve the right to make a final decision if consensus is not reached."[11] Public engagement strives for consensus (and sometimes achieves it), even though the prevailing power dynamic for most local government decisions does not require consensus as an outcome.

Element #5: Public engagement builds capacity for future engagement. It may seem obvious to point out that people learn to participate by participating. But it's true. Community members learn how to engage with local decisions by getting involved, showing up, trying things, failing, and sometimes succeeding. The same is true for local government agencies. Organizations learn how to design and implement public engagement by doing it. In that sense, implementing public engagement is the most effective way to build capacity for future public engagement.

Now more than ever, there is a significant need to build capacity for effective public engagement, not just among local government agencies, but also among the public. When participating in public decisions, community members and decision-makers learn how to discuss issues with people who may have different experiences and opinions. They learn how to collaborate and solve problems together. Public engagement helps communities strengthen networks and empowers community members to talk to each other, strengthen social networks, build social capital, and build trust with each other.

HOW TO USE THE CORE ELEMENTS

Let's put all the core elements together: (1) Public engagement is for public decisions, (2) is initiated by decision-makers, (3) involves shared influence, (4) strives for consensus, and (5) builds capacity. I use the core elements to help me in my practice any time I am approached to help a decision-maker, planner, or community implement a public engagement program. I use the core elements to help my clients and partners understand and articulate their true intentions. The purpose is to ensure we don't spread confusion to a community by inadvertently obscuring the real goals of public engagement or accidentally doing something else, such as public relations.

Before embarking on a public engagement program, ask the following questions:

1. Is there a public decision to be made?
2. Are decision-makers initiating the engagement?
3. Can the public influence the public decision?

The answers to these questions will help you quickly determine whether public engagement is the most appropriate course of action—and whether it's what you are really intended to do. If your answer is no to any of these questions, it is likely that public engagement is not appropriate. In some cases, such as when a decision can't be defined, or when there is not really a decision to be made, you may not be ready for public engagement. Likewise, if you discover that the public cannot have any influence over any aspect of a decision (maybe because the decision was already made), it may not be appropriate to ask for the public's input at all. The danger of asking for input when there is nothing in a decision the public can influence is that such activities could damage the public's trust and waste their time, which can hurt decision-makers' ability to engage the public in the future. It is imperative to help the public maintain realistic expectations about the process and how their input will impact the decision.

Many of my colleagues assert that public engagement should also be initiated by people who are not decision-makers, such as neighborhood organizations or members of the general public. Many believe that public engagement should be sustained and ongoing, even in the absence of a decision. Still others argue that members of the public shouldn't have to wait for their government to give them influence. And all those circumstances could have great benefit to society and democracy. But that is not the paradigm that most local-level planners and decision-makers operate in today. We work within structures that, for the most part, don't offer mechanisms that would allow us to conduct all public engagement activities on the right side of IAP2's Spectrum (Empower) or to give what Sherry Arnstein would call "Citizen Control." Having worked in this industry for two decades, I understand the realities of local and state government structures, policies, and power dynamics. Even practitioners who believe in policy mechanisms that provide citizen control and total government accountability are rarely able to make those structures a reality. But all is not lost. Part 2 of this book provides strategies that work with this existing power dynamic while helping you bring your public engagement activities closer to partnership, collaboration, and consensus.

KEY TAKEAWAYS

1. Public engagement is about sharing power in public decisions. If you discover that the public cannot have any influence over any aspect of

the decision at hand, it may not be appropriate to ask for the public's input at all.

2. Public engagement is a form of participatory democracy, which exists in a space somewhere between pure direct democracy and pure representative democracy.

3. The core elements of public engagement "in the wild" are:

- Public engagement is for public decisions.
- Public engagement is initiated by decision-makers.
- Public engagement involves (voluntarily) shared influence over the decision.
- Public engagement strives for consensus even though it is not always a required outcome. Consensus should not be confused with unanimity or majority vote.
- Public engagement builds the capacity to participate, among community members and public agencies.

NOTE

1. "Charette" is a French term to describe a multi-day design workshop, usually focused on a single idea, site, or neighborhood. The "World Café Method" is a small-group discussion technique conducted in multiple 20-minute rounds where small groups are presented with a different question to discuss in each round. Each round, it is prefaced with a different question for every small group to discuss. After the end of each round, participants leave that table and join a different table for the next round. "Participatory budgeting" is a process in which community members decide how to spend public dollars by proposing and developing ideas, and voting directly to fund projects.

REFERENCES

[1] American Planning Association's Professional Institute, *AICP Code of Ethics and Professional Conduct*. 205 N. Michigan Ave., Suite 1200 Chicago, IL 60601-59272021, American Institute of Certified Planners.

[2] Arnstein, S., A Ladder of Citizen Participation. *Journal of the American Planning Association*, 1969. **35**(4): pp. 216–224.

[3] Slotterback, C.S. and M. Lauria, Building a Foundation for Public Engagement in Planning: 50 Years of Impact, Interpretation, and Inspiration From Arnstein's Ladder. *Journal of the American Planning Association*, 2019. **85**(3): pp. 183–187.

[4] Bishop, P. and G. Davis, Mapping Public Participation in Policy Choices. *Australian Journal of Public Administration*, 2002. **61**: p. 18.

[5] Laurian, L. and M.M. Shaw, Evaluation of Public Participation: The Practices of Certified Planners. *Journal of Planning Education and Research*, 2009. **28**(3): pp. 293–309.

[6] Thomas, J.C., *Public Participation in Public Decisions: New Skills and Strategies for Public Managers.* 1st ed. Jossey-Bass public administration series. 1995, San Francisco: Jossey-Bass Publishers.

[7] Thomas, J.C., Public Involvement and Governmental Effectiveness: A Decision-Making Model for Public Managers. *Administration & Society,* 1993. **24**(4): pp. 444–469.

[8] International Association of Public Participation, *Foundations in Effective Public Participation: Planning for Effective Public Participation (Training Manual).* 2016. p. 165.

[9] Nabatchi, T. and M. Leighninger, *Public Participation for 21st Century Democracy.* 2015, Hoboken: John Wiley & Sons, Incorporated.

[10] Josey, A. *A Handbook for Consensus Decision-Making.* 2018 [cited 2023 September 5].

[11] Creighton, J.L., *The Public Participation Handbook: Making Better Decisions Through Citizen Involvement.* Hoboken, NJ, 2005. Jossey-Bass.

Four

INTRODUCTION

When things go wrong at a public meeting, it's easy to blame the public. We criticize the public for being "difficult" or for "grandstanding." We say the public just doesn't understand what we are trying to do. Maybe we write them off as paid protestors, claim they have a hidden agenda, or argue that they just aren't educated about the issue.

While all those things may be true, that does not change the fact that most of the time, when public engagement goes badly, it is not the public's fault. Rather, it is the result of poor planning and failing to set expectations. As practitioners we are sometimes our own worst enemies when it comes to implementing public engagement. The sheer complexity of the public engagement landscape offers plenty of opportunities to mess up.

Making mistakes is not the end of the world. It's how we learn. But the only way to learn from mistakes is to acknowledge that we are even making mistakes in the first place. I could fill an entire book with mistakes I have witnessed other convenors and facilitators make—and mistakes I have made myself.

Embarrassingly, I've made some mistakes more than once. Some of the most cringe-worthy errors I have made include forgetting to include key details about a meeting in a public invitation that I mailed to 3,000 residents, failing to confirm the date and time of a public meeting with the manager of a venue (only to arrive the night of the meeting to a locked door), and forgetting to bring pieces of audio-visual equipment to an important presentation.

But I have made different kinds of errors, too. These go beyond the kind of logistical details that are relatively easy to fix the next time. I have made the less obvious kinds of mistakes—the kind that stem from a lack of understanding about the meaning and goals of public engagement. This chapter distills these mistakes into four categories:

DOI: 10.4324/9781003451174-5

1. Engaging late
2. Involving without influence
3. Using data to (try to) persuade outraged people
4. Using bad techniques

ENGAGING LATE

Most public decision processes include many smaller decisions and milestones that add up to one, big decision. The more milestones we reach, the harder it is to consider new information—because that new information may require us to go backward and revisit milestones we already passed. Likewise, the more time that goes by in a project without engaging the public, the more milestones we reach before we engage the public. And the harder it becomes to incorporate public feedback into the decision. The more milestones we reach in a public decision process, *the harder it is for the public to have influence in the decision.* And when we engage too late in a decision process, we put ourselves in a defensive position. If we reach the end of a decision process without engaging the public, we have narrowed our options to two: (1) defend the decision at all costs or (2) revise the decision, at considerable expense.

Late engagement puts decision-makers in a defensive position, often referred to as the "decide-announce-defend" model (or a DAD). The DAD method has historically been used by federal agencies in the context of nuclear waste disposal siting.[1] The more often decision-makers use a DAD, the less trusting the public becomes of the decision process. The less trusting the public becomes, the more antagonistic future decision processes become. As decisions become antagonistic, decision-makers come to expect hostility from the public and come to fear the public's response to *any* decision. Decision-makers can begin to question the merit of asking the public to participate in decisions at all. At this stage, decision-makers are more likely to convince themselves that the public is irrational, uneducated, unqualified, and difficult. Decision-makers lean toward secrecy and stonewalling, hoping the less information they share about decisions, the less the public will know, and the less public anger, protest, or legal appeal will exist. And the cycle continues.

The ability for the public to influence a decision through participatory methods declines as a decision process reaches more milestones toward a final decision. We can visualize this dynamic and the effects of late engagement in a graph format (Figure 4.1). The public's ability to influence a decision through participatory methods starts out at its highest at

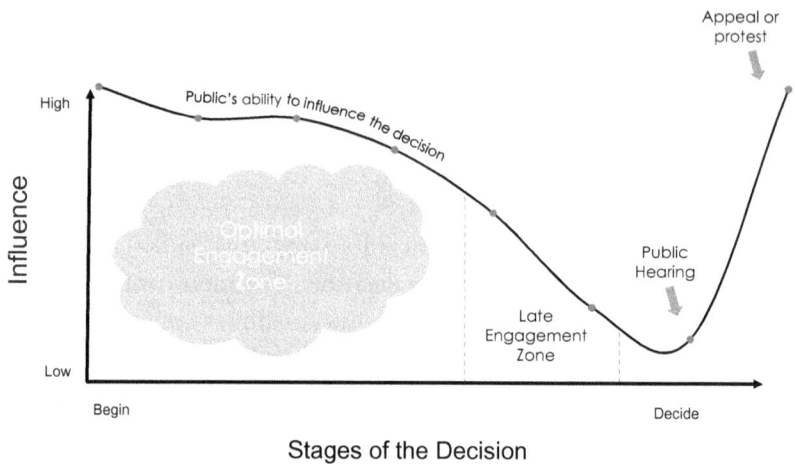

Figure 4.1 Optimal engagement zone.

the very beginning of a decision process and then declines throughout the process, making a steep dive to its lowest right before a final decision. The public's level of influence through participatory means is usually lowest in the moments leading up to a final decision. But the public's ability to influence the decision by other means then spikes once the decision is made, which is the point in the process where legal options become available, such as an appeal. But there is a significant difference in the type and tenor of influence during the pre- and post-decision time periods. As one community member told me, "If you're not going to invite us into the decision process, we will have no choice but to force our way in."

Before a final decision is made, decision-makers have a greater opportunity to share influence with the public through sponsored, participatory methods. Toward the end of a decision process, the public's desire (or need) to influence the decision using non-participatory methods, such as protest, increases. Post-decision, the opportunity to share influence through participatory methods is lost. Influence shifts completely to non-participatory methods, such as appeals, and other legal remedies intended to reverse decisions.

Engaging late is one of the biggest mistakes practitioners make. Engaging early is not a guarantee that we will reach consensus and sail through a decision without delay. But the later we engage the public, the more likely we are to face surprises later and the more likely the public will mobilize its influence using non-participatory methods, such as lobbying, protest, and legal appeals. The circumstances created by late engagement can result in project delay and additional expense (to the public agency and community members). Perhaps the most damaging consequence of late engagement is the loss of public trust.

ENGAGEMENT WITHOUT INFLUENCE

Most of the time when an engagement program fails to share influence, it is a function of late engagement. As we learned in the previous section, the later in a decision process, the less influence there is to share. But even when practitioners set out to engage the public early, the concept of shared influence is left out of the equation.

There can be a temptation to pursue a public engagement program even when there are no opportunities for public influence. An engagement program can include many techniques that look like opportunities for influence—such as surveys, town hall meetings, and workshops—even when they are not sharing influence at all. Doing this feels safer than admitting to the public there is no opportunity for influence. The consequences of doing that, however, can be costly. Involvement without influence can create frustration among the public and staff.[2]

Involvement without influence can be seen as a waste of the public's time, as placation, or worse: manipulation. Involvement without influence can erode the public trust in decision-making.

It is also easy to lose sight of shared influence when we throw our efforts into making a public engagement program fun and interactive, for instance to make a public meeting feel more like a party. The party planning can overshadow the real work of identifying our objectives and stating clearly why we want to engage the public in the first place.

I must admit that I have been a major offender of the "party planning" approach to engagement. One is easily lulled into the magic of a fun event where there is no conflict or tough discussions. But public engagement events designed to look like a party can too easily become a form of performative engagement. Performative engagement is something we do to make it appear as though our event is inclusive, and meaningful—when in fact, we either don't know our objectives, or we're masking a lack of transparency around the decision (more on how to achieve transparency in Chapter 7).

A party makes for a great press release, but does it achieve any engagement objectives? Were people informed? Did they understand the decision and who is making it? Did they understand their influence in the decision? Did they understand what specifically was being asked of them and how their feedback would be used? When we are too focused on planning a party, the answer to these questions can easily become "no."

A member of the public summed this up for me a few years ago as he exited a public meeting I had helped plan. He said,

> No one is fooled because they walk away from a public meeting with cookies and a free pen. The public doesn't need their government to throw them a party. They need their government to make decisions in a transparent way.

USING DATA TO (TRY TO) CONVINCE OUTRAGED PEOPLE

Oftentimes when my clients have engaged late and then designed engagement without meaningful influence, they find themselves backed into a corner. Being too late in the decision process to revisit key milestones or undo work that has already been completed, decision-makers are left with few options except to prepare the lawyers and hope the public will support the decision. This precarious position leads many decision-makers to conclude the only way to avoid public protest or appeal is to *sell* the public on the merits of the decision. That is usually when I get a call and I'm asked to "engage" the community by developing talking points and messaging that will convince the public the decision is good for them. This is usually a public relations campaign disguised as public engagement.

There is a time and a place for education, public relations, and for presenting data that support a decision. But the time to do that is not at the end of a decision process or when members of the public are concerned, upset, or angry. Many planners and public decision-makers insist that the most effective way to deal with community outrage is to patiently present objective facts and data about the decision at hand. My clients often say to me, "We just need to educate the public." Others reason, "If people just hear the facts, then they will agree with this decision and they can't be outraged."

Combating outrage with facts and figures is like fighting a fire with gasoline. It is not effective and only makes the situation worse. The scientific community agrees that facts don't convince people who are emotionally charged. The well-documented phenomenon of confirmation bias causes us to undervalue evidence that contradicts our beliefs—and overvalue evidence that confirms our beliefs.[3] This effect is further exacerbated when we are in an agitated, fearful, and emotional state. It is thought that because complex information is cognitively taxing, people instead take mental "shortcuts."[4] Confirmation bias is a subconscious method we use to minimize our emotional distress. None of us wants to find out we are wrong about something, let alone when we already feel threatened and afraid. No amount of evidence will sink in when a person is in a heightened negative emotional state.

Research shows that people are more receptive to being influenced when they are calm and relaxed, as opposed to feeling stressed or threatened.[5] By contrast, when people feel their beliefs and values are being threatened, they will defend them. At that point, everyone is less capable of having an evidence-based discussion, no matter how much data are presented. Don't believe me? Consider how you felt the last time you engaged in a debate about gun control, abortion, or anti-racism. When faced with information that feels threatening to our beliefs and values, most of us become less willing or able to accept information presented by the decision-makers, no matter how "convincing" that information was deemed to be.

Unfortunately, most public engagement efforts—and public meetings—are organized in direct contradiction to these findings on human nature. A typical public meeting begins with a long, fact-filled presentation designed around the myth that facts change minds. Such a presentation sends a signal to the audience that the convenors and facilitators believe what they are saying is more important than anything the public could say.

If members of the public came to a meeting because they were already upset about the decision, they are unlikely to be convinced otherwise, even by compelling factual information. This is especially true when meeting organizers ask the public to sit through a long presentation and only offer a chance for attendees to share their ideas and concerns afterwards. The irony is that, even as more information is presented, less of that information can be processed in the conscious brains of participants. The more complex the information, the more likely that information is to be processed in the same parts of the brain that process fear.[4]

During a technical presentation, participants are not just soaking up the information, happily changing their minds, or wondering what other data might prove them wrong. Participants are more likely to spend that time disagreeing with what is being presented and formulating arguments to refute whatever doesn't align with their beliefs. We all do this. The emotional center of our brain takes over. That is why, without an outlet built in, our meetings (and entire engagement processes) can get bogged down with unacknowledged emotions, concerns, fears, hopes, and desires. Left for too long, these unacknowledged emotions will overwhelm a meeting or an entire public engagement process.

A more effective way to share information is to first seek common ground. Explore people's beliefs, values, concerns, and hopes *before* presenting facts and figures about a controversial topic. I share more about why and how this works using a technique called Productive Venting in Chapter 11.

WEAK TECHNIQUES

Even if a particular technique is not successful at a given time, very few participation techniques are inherently bad. Weak techniques are simply those that are used at the wrong time and in the wrong context. The same technique used in the right context can be effective. That said, there are a handful of techniques that are difficult to get right, no matter the timing, or the context.

In public engagement, a technique describes the tactics and methods used to carry out an engagement program. Examples of techniques include newsletters, public meetings, online surveys, one-on-one interviews, and workshops. There is an additional layer of techniques used to help facilitate meetings and other gatherings, such as icebreakers and various group discussion exercises.

There are hundreds of useful public engagement techniques at our disposal. And yet, most of us employ just a handful of techniques. The top three most frequently used engagement techniques are open houses, town hall meetings, and public hearings. There are many reasons that planners and decision-makers are limited to these three techniques, including regulatory requirements and a variety of misconceptions I discuss in the next chapter.

The techniques I describe below may not be bad in all contexts. But they are often a challenge to use effectively. For that reason, they should be used only after careful consideration—and should be coordinated with a larger public engagement program to avoid over-reliance on weak techniques.

Open houses

An open house is a variation of a public meeting that usually has no set agenda, no formal presentation, and no facilitated discussion. Some describe an open house as a "buffet style" meeting where people can drop in anytime to review project information at booths or stations, and talk one-on-one with experts, convenors, and decision-makers.

Open houses are a beloved technique among many planners and decision-makers. Fans of this technique will say the flexible and casual environment is more comfortable for attendees than a more formal setting and that it offers a more direct connection with decision-makers. Others say it is a good way to break up complex information into multiple stations, allowing people to gravitate toward whichever aspect of the project is most interesting to them.

There is another view of open houses. Open houses can provide a false sense of security to the convenors. There is a perception that open houses are safe way to protect experts and decision-makers from the public's prying questions, unreasonable demands, or outrage. The so-called informal format is also a convenient way to diffuse conflict or tension; it is harder for the public to disrupt an open house than a regular public meeting. Many of my colleagues lean on open houses, especially when there is expected controversy about an issue, to avoid conflict.

But if there is potential controversy and concern about how to public will react to a particular initiative, an open house will not solve the controversy. An open house will likely push the problem down the road. The format of an open house reduces the opportunity for community members to share their concerns about a project as part of a meaningful dialogue. During an open house, the public may happen across a member of the project team who can answer their questions. But to share ideas, concerns or provide other feedback, members of the public will be instructed to fill out a comment card. It is unlikely there will be opportunities for dialogue. An open house does not provide a sense of accountability; anything said to one or two staff members at an open house won't be heard by other members of the public or necessarily documented in the record. Not having a meaningful outlet for the public's concerns doesn't mean those concerns go away. It means those concerns are more likely to grow and come up later in the decision process as surprises and outrage.

Over the years, community members have told me open houses feel designed to prevent dialogue and accountability. The room feels like it is designed to disperse attendees on purpose to control the crowd and ensure community members don't gather, discuss, or collaborate. Others have told me they feel alienated and excluded by open houses because they are afraid to ask the experts "dumb" questions. Others have expressed frustration with the reliance on comment cards or sticky notes in place of true dialogue. One open house attendee told me, "It feels like whenever someone doesn't want to answer a question, they tell me to write it on a sticky note. But does anyone ever read those? It feels very flimsy."

Open houses are not an inherently bad technique, but without careful thought, their overuse can cause decision-makers to miss important feedback that can resurface later in a decision process. An open house is best used toward the end of a decision process, when presenting final plans or documents to the public that require only small clarifications and very minor feedback.

Town hall-style meetings

Town hall-style meetings are among the most common types of public meetings in the US. Still, I urge my clients to avoid them at all costs. Unlike open houses, which can be deployed in limited circumstances, town hall meetings achieve very little in the way of productive dialogue or problem-solving. The structure and format of town hall meetings prevents real deliberation and dialogue, meaning that even a "well-executed" town hall meeting will disappoint participants won't feel heard and convenors will feel mistreated.

When we think of town hall meetings today, what most often comes to mind is a format used for presidential debates. Yet, this is a relatively new iteration of a town hall that emerged in the late 1980s and early 1990s. Town hall meetings originated during the colonial era. The original New England town halls date back to the 1600s, where townspeople (read: white male property owners) voted directly to decide all the town's official matters.

In addition to presidential debates, modern day town hall-style meetings are held in local communities across the country. Today's town hall-style meetings, however, are only loosely based on the original. Participants in today's town hall meetings do not actually vote or make legally binding decisions. Instead, today's town halls are hosted by politicians to meet with and allow their constituents to voice an opinion. A variation of this format has been adopted by local leaders across the US as the default form of public engagement. Town hall-style meetings are even used by private companies to share information with employees.

Town hall-style meetings make headlines, especially when the convenors of said meetings are yelled at, taunted, or shouted down by angry crowds. In many places, the town halls have led to fistfights and even arrests.

The chaos we see at town halls is not entirely the public's fault. The fault is, in part, due to the format itself and the decision to use it. But if any of us were asked, we would be challenged to describe what a town hall is exactly. What is its purpose? How is it structured? The purported purpose is to give community members the chance to voice their opinions. But to what end? The dysfunction of a town hall meeting is, in part, a function of its nebulous definition that allows many local officials adapt it in self-serving ways. What kind of meeting is a town hall actually? What can people expect when they attend one? Many of us cannot answer those questions.

The general lack of purpose and structure is compounded by the typical choice of venue for a town hall and how the room is arranged. Almost every town hall meeting I have attended or seen on TV has been hosted in a council or board chamber or auditorium that is ill equipped to handle the crowd (too big or too small) or the intended activity (discussion). The convenors of the meeting usually sit at front of the room, on a stage, or behind a dais or large table, while participants are asked to sit in rows of folding chairs, or in seats affixed to the floor, or in benches arranged like pews. This arrangement reinforces the power dynamic between decision-makers and the public—and signals to participants that their role is to observe and obey, not to collaborate or share influence over a decision.

The second challenge with town hall meetings is the typical structure and the typical agenda. Town hall meetings rarely offer structured opportunities for participants to connect with each other, converse with each other, learn from each other—or otherwise build rapport before or during the meeting. When the meeting is called to order, there may be introductory remarks that identify the issue that prompted the meeting or to establish baseline of shared information. If the convenors have prepared a presentation, it is often far too lengthy. When the meeting is opened for comments, participants who wish to voice an opinion about the topic must stand in front of the entire audience and address decision-makers from a microphone, one at a time.

Town hall-style meetings are intended to maximize the quantity of participation. But they even fail at that. A key failing of a town hall meeting is its lack of efficiency. If ten people attend a town hall, it is possible that each person would have a chance to speak. But with such low attendance, that meeting would be considered a failure. If 150 people attend that same town hall meeting, we would call that a good turnout. But consider the proportion of attendees who would be able to speak at that meeting. Even if the entire two-hour meeting were devoted solely to public comment, at most there would be enough time to hear from 30 to 40 people. At the end of the ordeal, we still wouldn't know what 75 percent of participants thought about the issue, or why they even came to the meeting.

Members of the public have come to expect this course of events, where they are not provided an opportunity to comment at all. People in communities across the US have learned to come prepared to a town hall meeting with homemade signs saying things like, "Disagree!"

Attempts to end a contentious town hall meeting on time are often unsuccessful. With no facilitator to bring the meeting to a close or even an agenda to consult, the end time can be extended by a grumbling or shouting crowd whose members feel snubbed. This leaves many participants in the awkward position of trying to escape out the back just so they can go home and eat dinner. Others may trickle out of the room as they reach their personal limits, leaving the town hall in same state of confusion they started with. When the town hall does finally stagger to the end, participants may look around and see that only a third of the crowd is still there. There is no applause, no sense of shared values or common purpose, and no sense of accomplishment. There is milling and grumbling. That includes the people who organized and hosted the meeting, who are likely worn out, anxious, and infuriated themselves.

There is never an appropriate context for a town hall-style meeting. Their use is usually a sign that the convenors haven't identified their purpose and objectives. Instead of using town halls, I urge my clients and partners to choose from dozens of other, better techniques. Chapters 9, 10, and 11 describe how to choose more effective techniques.

Public hearings

Over the course of my career, I've attended countless public hearings. Many are hopelessly long and dull. Some are confusing and tense. Others are dangerous. What all hearings have in common is their unpredictability. *How many people will show up? Will it be the same ten people who always come out to oppose decisions? What will they think of this proposal? Will people* be angry? What if people protest? Will the meeting go all night? Will the decision get squashed? Will we have to spend thousands of dollars to redesign this project?

Many of my clients believe that the pain of public hearings is a fact of life in local government.

There will always be those people who just want to oppose everything, right?

I've spent years watching and listening to people who oppose local government decisions. The typical complaints are more often about the public hearing process than the substance of the decision at hand. Community members often say things like, "I support this idea, but I just don't like the way you went about it."

Public hearings are a feature of the legal system. A public hearing is a formal meeting where members of the public give official comments about a decision, either spoken or written. The meeting is usually recorded and transcribed in order to create a legal record. Public hearings are defined by formal, procedural rules and requirements. They are highly scripted and choreographed, which can make them feel bureaucratic and confusing. According to James L. Creighton, the founding president of IAP2 and author of several books on public engagement, the primary purpose of public hearings is to "serve lawyers" and they should be avoided except where legally required.[6]

Due to their legal nature, public hearings are not designed to be an effective form of public engagement. We can't squeeze months' worth of public engagement into one procedural hearing. But that is precisely what local government officials are asked to do all the time.

There is also the issue of timing I described earlier in this chapter. Attempts engage the public at a hearing come too late. By the time we hold a public hearing, it's possible that months—or years—worth of work has already been done. At that point, it is often highly challenging to accept meaningful feedback on a project, as it would cost time and money to make changes at such a late stage. Public officials find themselves in a sort of Catch-22, where they are required to seek feedback at exactly the moment in the decision process when getting feedback is most risky.

A public hearing occurs at the end of a decision but is often the first-time members of the public learn about the decision. The public might have received a notice in the mail, or heard about it from a neighbor, or read about on social media. The public hearing might be the public's only opportunity to learn more about a project and provide feedback. The public notice may even have said "give us your input" or "provide comments." And so the public's expectation is that this is their chance to influence the decision. This is why the timing of public hearings is so problematic: We ask for public feedback at the exact moment we are least able to accept it.

Am I suggesting we get rid of hearings? No. As described above, public hearings are required by law and serve an important purpose. But given the challenges the format presents, public hearings should always be part of a larger public engagement program to ensure that members of the public have a chance to participate long before the decision reaches its final stages.

Meeting in auditoriums

During the initial COVID-19 pandemic lockdowns of 2020, planners and local leaders across the US had to completely rethink how to engage the public. Local and state restrictions on in-person gatherings, coupled with requirements for social distancing meant that most in-person meetings, especially in school auditoriums, were off limits. These restrictions caused many of us to step back and reflect on why we ever hosted meetings in auditoriums in the first place.

Auditoriums are not designed for interaction and collaboration. They are made for concerts and speeches. Auditoriums are designed to maximize performance, a one-way form of communication, which requires a quiet, passive audience. Talking, coughing, or making other noise when seated in an auditorium violates powerful social norms that are reinforced by the design. Let's consider the ways in which auditoriums are designed to prevent interaction among people.

- The seats in the audience are affixed to the ground, in long rows of 20 or more and it's challenging for participants to move around the room or get in and out of seats.
- Audience members can't see each other because they are cloaked in darkness. Lighting is designed to illuminate the stage (and often remains that way because no one can ever find the switch for the house lights).
- The stage is set higher than the audience, so the people speaking (usually representatives of the decision-makers) are separated and literally above the participants.

- The acoustics are designed to amplify the sounds coming from the stage, while muffling the sounds coming from the audience.

The design of an auditorium makes it challenging to encourage interaction between people at a public meeting, let alone hold a collaborative discussion. The people on stage can't see when audience members raise their hands with a question. Without a microphone, audience members' voices are absorbed into acoustical panels. If a microphone has been installed at the end of the aisle, those who wish to speak must get up out of their seats, squeeze by others in their row, walk down the aisle, and speak into a microphone, one at a time. If more than a few people want to speak or ask a question during the meeting, they must form a line in the aisle. Like the cramped line to the bathroom in an airplane aisle, this is not appreciated by anyone with an aisle seat.

And the worst insult to participants is that they can't even talk to each other. The occasional whisper may be tolerated. But talking to the person seated next to you feels wrong—because it *is* wrong in that setting. The layout, the seats, the lighting, the stage—it is all designed to make people face forward and pay attention to the stage, not to interact with each other.

When we hold a meeting in an auditorium, we signal to participants that we don't really care what they have to say. If we truly wanted input, feedback, or discussion, then why host a meeting in a room that is least hospitable to this goal? An auditorium would be perfect if our goal was to give a performance or a speech. But if our goal is simply to share information, we must ask ourselves, do we really need to make people to sit in an auditorium for that? Do we need to convene people at all for that purpose? In most cases, people can find that information online. Or read it in an email.

The danger of hosting public meetings in auditoriums is that it's easy to assume the lack of discussion means participants are in agreement with an initiative—or don't care. But silence is not consensus. Often at public meetings in auditoriums, people don't speak up because it was too difficult or uncomfortable.

Due to the reasons I describe above, I do not recommend that any local leader attempt to host a public meeting, workshop, or hearing in an auditorium. Almost any other community space, such as a cafeteria, gymnasium, lobby, or large classroom would provide a better experience—and a more welcoming and productive atmosphere.

KEY TAKEAWAYS

This chapter reviews some of the most damaging mistakes we make and bad techniques we use when designing and implementing public engagement. To recap:

1. **Engaging late** increases the chances that decision-makers will face surprises during the decision process that could result in project delay, additional expense, and loss of public trust.
2. **Engaging the public without sharing influence** can create frustration among the public, erode public trust in decision-making, and waste people's time.
3. **Using data to convince outraged people.** Due to built-in cognitive biases, emotionally charged people are rarely convinced by data and facts.
4. **Techniques,** such as open houses, town hall-style meetings, and any meetings in auditoriums, are challenging to use in most contexts and should be used sparingly, if at all.

REFERENCES

[1] Blowers, A., What Happened When DAD Met LULU: Decide, Announce, Defend was the Old Way of Selecting Waste Sites, But It Didn't Work with Locally Unwanted Land Use. Andrew Blowers on a New Approach. *New Statesman* (1996), 2003. **132**(4657): p. viii.
[2] Thomas, J.C., Public Involvement and Governmental Effectiveness: A Decision-Making Model for Public Managers. *Administration & Society*, 1993. **24**(4): pp. 444–469.
[3] Kahneman, D., *Thinking, Fast and Slow*. 1st ed. 2011, New York: Farrar, Straus and Giroux.
[4] Toomey, A.H., Why Facts Don't Change Minds: Insights from Cognitive Science for the Improved Communication of Conservation Research. *Biological Conservation*, 2023. **278**: p. 109886.
[5] Pandey, S. and R. Gupta, *Book Review: The Influential Mind: What the Brain Reveals About Our Power to Change Others*. 2019. Frontiers Research Foundation, United Kingdom.
[6] Creighton, J.L., *The Public Participation Handbook: Making Better Decisions Through Citizen Involvement*. Hoboken, NJ. 2005. Jossey-Bass.

Five

Common objections

INTRODUCTION

In previous chapters, we learned what public engagement is, the mistakes we make, and the consequences when it all goes sideways. This chapter unpacks all the reason *why* not everyone wants to do it, why we make mistakes and use weak techniques even though such actions often run counter to our goals, values, and ethics as planners. While many of us are motivated by the desire to improve local decisions, bring greater involvement and equity to local policies and plans, and improve the quality of life for all community members, we still grapple with our own fears and skepticism about involving the public in local decisions.

One of the biggest challenges of my work over the last decade has been convincing decision-makers to engage the public at all. I have often wondered if my experience is unique, whether I was approaching it all wrong, working with the wrong clients, or in the wrong part of the country. But when I was researching this book, I discovered a widespread skepticism of public engagement among policymakers. As I noted in the introduction to this book: a major problem with public engagement is that so many practitioners don't want to do it. If that sentiment describes you, you're not alone.

Many planners and decision-makers share similar, negative sentiments about public engagement. In the face of our lived experiences, the benefits of public engagement are not always obvious. What's more, not everyone is aware of the empirical research showing us concrete, beneficial outcomes. For these reasons, it can be challenging to convince decision-makers to engage the public in a meaningful way.

Research shows that decision-makers' attitudes about engagement play a significant role in the overall success of public engagement activities. Because decision-makers are part of the design and implementation of public engagement, their attitudes are predictors of how participatory

DOI: 10.4324/9781003451174-6

processes are designed and how much influence the public may have in a particular decision.[1]

There are a variety of factors that influence how decision-makers view public engagement. On an individual level, there are personal characteristics that influence decision-makers' attitudes, such as their sense of civic duty, their overall job satisfaction, their prior experiences with public engagement, whether they trust the public, have long-term relationships with the community, and whether they have skills in listening and conflict resolution. It also matters what kind of organization decision-makers represent. Agencies with more decision-making autonomy and discretion tend to need public support and legitimacy, thus selecting for managers that favor public engagement.

By contrast, organizations with red tape, bureaucratic requirements, and hierarchical structures can negatively impact how managers and decision-makers view public engagement. These rigid organizational characteristics can make it challenging for public managers and decision-makers to implement public engagement processes, which, by design, carry uncertainty that could potentially disrupt an organization's strict rules. Finally, there are procedural factors that impact how decision-makers view public engagement. Research shows that decision-makers prefer procedural clarity and early engagement. That is, having rules and fixed boundaries around engagement made the whole process more attractive to decision-makers.[1]

The way decision-makers view public engagement can have a major impact on how and when (or even if) public engagement occurs. Attitudes about public engagement are highly complex and dependent upon individual traits, organizational cultures, and larger community contexts. I share this research because understanding how public managers and decision-makers view public engagement can help us better understand some of the most cited objections.

The objections I share in the following paragraphs originate from years of helping clients and partners design public engagement programs—and hearing many of these objections from them. I believe that understanding these objections will allow you to better explore your own skepticism as well as respond to objections from others.

Many objections I hear stem from a general skepticism of public engagement:

Why we even bother engaging the public at all?

Isn't it just a time consuming and expensive way to find out what we already know?

The public are ignorant of the facts.

Shouldn't public decisions be left to the experts?

Shouldn't public decisions be left to the people who were elected to make them?

To help understand the various objections to public engagement, I've organized them into the following most common themes:

1. Public engagement is expensive and time consuming.
2. The public is not qualified to be part of the decision.
3. Public officials were elected to make these decisions, not the public.
4. We already know what the public thinks.
5. Engaging the public means handing a decision over to them.
6. Public engagement stirs the pot.
7. The public has "meeting fatigue."

OBJECTION #1: PUBLIC ENGAGEMENT IS EXPENSIVE AND TIME CONSUMING

In 1995, an organization called America Speaks burst onto the public engagement landscape with an ambitious mission to "reinvigorate American Democracy by engaging citizens in the public decision-making that most impacts their lives."[2] The organization developed and trademarked a method, known as 21st Century Town Meetings, in which anywhere from 500 to 5,000 participants gathered in one single forum to discuss a particular issue or decision. The 21st Century Town Meeting method has been used for many high-profile, national policy efforts, including a nationwide discussion of Social Security, which engaged 45,000 people, and an effort entitled "Listening to the City" held in New York City to engage almost 5,000 residents about redevelopment of the World Trade Center site.

What is a 21st Century Town Meeting? Picture a convention center exhibit hall set up with a stage, big screens, the room filled with dozens of large, round tables, each equipped with flip charts, markers, facilitator guides, and maps. Elected officials and community leaders are in attendance. There is palpable excitement in the air, as attendees collaborate with fellow community members—all together in one place to help solve a problem or question.

These kinds of meetings are exciting and impactful. They happen to be bog, prolonged efforts, conducted by multiple entities. They engage thousands of community members and cost tens or hundreds of thousands of dollars.

The 21st Century Town Meeting model is cited in numerous case studies and publications about public engagement. It is inspiring. But it is also daunting for the typical practitioner. Many ask, is this how public engagement is supposed to be? To achieve something like that would take months to plan, a staff of event planners and facilitators, a budget to rent the convention center, and even more money to provide catering and drinks. The cost of this seems unreachable for many local government planners and decision-makers in the US.

For these reasons, I am not surprised that one of the most common objections I hear from decision-makers is that public engagement costs too much. They have an image not unlike America Speaks, of huge convention halls filled with people. They think that quality participation means making a splash—and that requires a dedicated team of dozens of people and a big budget.

It's true that public engagement *can* be expensive. And in a perfect world, we might devote the resources necessary to replicate an America Speaks 21st Century Town Meeting for most of our public decisions. But public engagement does not have to be implemented at that scale every time. It does not have to be expensive.

I know I'm not fooling anyone into thinking public engagement costs nothing. There will invariably be *some* cost. But consider there are multiple ways to think about cost. One way to think about cost is to consider the cost of doing the engagement activity itself, which may include things like sending mail, purchasing supplies and equipment, subscribing to digital engagement tools, hiring consultants, and hosting meetings. An agency can spend tens or hundreds of thousands of dollars on a public engagement program. And yes, it can be expensive. But compared to what? Compared to doing nothing? When we are tallying up the cost of engaging the public, we rarely compare the cost of a modest public engagement plan to the cost of the alternative—of doing public engagement badly, or not doing it at all.

This leads us to the second way to think about cost, which is what economists refer to as opportunity cost. An opportunity cost is the benefit we give up when choosing to do one thing instead of another thing. A classic example of opportunity cost is a college student who spends four hours and $30 playing video games and ordering pizza the night before an important exam. The opportunity cost of that evening was not just the $30. The opportunity costs were twofold: (1) the cost of the time not spent studying for the important exam, thus impacting the student's future and (2) the cost of not putting that $30 into a savings account that would achieve compound growth over the next several decades.

In a situation in which a decision-maker elects to forgo public engagement, or to do the minimum required public engagement activities, the opportunity cost refers to the benefits lost from that choice. This is the cost incurred when the lack of participation or poorly executed participation motivates members of the public to oppose and protest a decision. In that case, the chances of a project being delayed, forced into a redesign/re-write, or getting scuttled entirely go up quickly. The cost of revising a decision that has already been made can be higher than the cost of engaging the public in the first place.

Consider the example of a town board that has engaged an engineering consultant to design a new configuration for Main Street. This is a town of 12,000 residents, where the board members are volunteers and the budget to pay the engineer has come through a grant from the state. The resources to engage the community, they say, simply do not exist. Rather than spending the time, effort, and budget to engage the community and seek feedback on the design of Main Street, the town leaders forgo any public outreach, saying that if members of the public have any feedback, they can provide comment during the public hearing.

After six months of working with a consulting engineer, the town is finally ready to approve the design and move forward on construction. In fact, grant that the town received to pay for the design and construction requires that the town reach design milestones by certain dates to release the funds for construction. With three weeks remaining on the first big milestone, the town schedules a public hearing. On the night of the public hearing, hundreds of community members show up to express their concerns. Many are upset that they had not heard about this important project before that evening. Others in attendance are people who own businesses along Main Street and whose driveways and parking will be directly impacted by the design. A group from an influential senior citizens organization also came to the meeting. They pointed out that the design featured very few accommodations for seniors and people with disabilities. Other members of the community came out to support of their friends and neighbors.

Over the course of the evening, the board hears from dozens of people who express confusion, anger, and outrage about the project. It becomes clear that this is not a politically expedient decision for members of the town board. The community is splintered by an unpopular decision. Without any clear sense of public support, board members fear for their political futures. So, they vote to table the decision until more public feedback can be sought. This means the town must scramble to organize a separate public meeting to get feedback, then ask the consulting engineer to revise the design (at considerable expense), and risk not meeting the important milestone to activate state grant funding, which means that the town could lose the funding for the construction altogether.

That is the opportunity cost of not doing public engagement. What could have been prevented by spending time and money may have cost the entire project. It can be much more expensive to redesign a project that was tabled due to public protest than it would have been to engage the community in the first place.

The misconception that public engagement is too expensive is understandable when some of the most visible case studies come out of impressive initiatives like America Speaks. Not all public engagement needs to be implemented on a grand scale like that. Nor do we have to engage thousands of participants for the participation to be legitimate. In many cases, particularly in smaller communities, a more focused and targeted outreach effort can be just as inclusive and effective as a stadium event (more on this in Chapter 9).

Waiting too long in the project timeline to engage the community, or not engaging at all, are two scenarios that are more likely to slow down a project than the engagement itself. Those are the two conditions in which public opposition is most likely to emerge. The further we move along in a project timeline, the more milestones we reach, the more small decisions we make that will be more time consuming to change later. Absent a thorough engagement process, public opposition can (and does) arise at unpredictable moments in the decision process, usually after planners and local officials have already made a significant investment of time and money in a project.

Public engagement will always take time to design and implement. I am not here to sell you "hack" that will cut the time in half. Having practiced public engagement for many years, I know it can take weeks or months just to prepare your internal team, let alone the additional time needed to design, plan, and coordinate logistics for a single public event (and time needed to plan an entire program that involves multiple touch points with the public).

But we can think differently about the time we do have available to us during a decision process, how we use that time as we reach new milestones in our decision, and how public engagement activities can align with our decision process to ensure that we are not creating a build-up of unmet needs, anger, outrage, and potentially big delays. A small investment early in the process can produce big rewards later in the form of saved time and expense.

OBJECTION #2: THE PUBLIC IS NOT QUALIFIED TO INFLUENCE THIS DECISION

In many cases, public officials' attitudes about public engagement are influenced by how competent they think the public is. Many public officials believe that public decisions should be left to the experts. In fact, studies show that many public managers do not trust the public to be competent enough to participate—and many officials believe that lack of expertise among the public is a major barrier to involving them.[3] This is one reason why my clients and partners often tell me it is impossible to involve the public in highly technical decisions.

Local government decisions are often highly complex and technical, involving policy, engineering, architecture, financial analysis, and construction. *How could we possibly involve regular people in these complex decisions*, we say? The public are not experts in the technical design of a parking garage, or the modeling a flood plain, or calculating the financial feasibility of a community ice-skating rink. Laypeople are not usually familiar with how to design a compound curve for a street intersection or how to select the type of structural steel to use in the construction of a parking garage. For everyone's safety, we should let certified experts do those analyses, create designs, and make recommendations. Our responsibility is to ensure the public's health and safety by ensuring properly designed public infrastructure.

But that doesn't mean complex decisions should be left entirely to the experts. As James Creighton points out in *The Public Participation Handbook*, "experts cannot make decisions without assigning a weight or priority to competing values that society believes are good," noting that decisions about whether a safety risk is acceptable or how much is reasonable to pay for a new facility are not technical decisions, "even if they involve a great deal of technical information."[4]

The question of expertise in public decision-making can be unraveled in two parts. First, hidden within every seemingly technical decision are layers of non-technical factors, such as public preferences, needs, and values. Just because certain aspects of a decision are best left to experts does not mean the *entire decision* should be left to experts. Sure, it may be inappropriate to ask the public to decide whether to use pre-cast or cast-in-place concrete in the construction of a parking garage. But there are many aspects of the decision the public can influence. The public can be involved in the selection of a site as well as numerous aspects of the design, such as lighting, safety features, the use of ground floor space, the look and feel of materials on the external façade, the presence of amenities such as bicycle facilities, and features to enhance accessibility for children, seniors, and people with disabilities. Highly complex decisions can almost always be broken down into less complicated elements. And it is usually those less complicated elements that the public cares about the most. Members of the public are likely to trust the experts to handle the engineering. But the public does not always trust the engineers to decide everything else, especially aspects of a decision that express public needs and values.

The second assumption we should question is the very notion that the public are not qualified. Sure, many members of the public may not be engineers or architects (although many are). One thing is always true: the public *are* experts in their own lived experience. And in many cases, that lived experience can contribute value to a public decision. Someone who lives near the proposed parking garage may know a lot about how traffic circulates and have an intuitive understanding of the demand for parking throughout the week. While that person may not have the technical vocabulary, that person may have a tremendous amount of insight to share with the experts who will be selecting a site and designing the garage. Likewise, people who operate businesses along the same street may have insights into what kind of ground floor uses would be most welcome and what kind of façade design would complement the character of the neighborhood. Members of the disability community would likely bring lived expertise to the question of how best to provide accessibility for people with physical and intellectual disabilities. These are aspects of a highly complex and technical decision in which the public *can* provide expertise.

Just because there are aspects of a decision that should be left to experts does not mean every aspect of the decision needs to be—nor should it be. Even for highly complex and technical decisions, it is possible (and advisable) to find pieces of the decision that would benefit from the public's lived experience—and expertise.

OBJECTION #3: THE PUBLIC WASN'T ELECTED TO MAKE THESE DECISIONS. WE WERE

This objection is not just another version of the "unqualified public" complaint. There is an important distinction: this objection is less about whether the public is qualified, and more about how someone interprets democratic principles. Many local elected officials believe the whole point of being elected is to make decisions on behalf of the people who voted. The public voted—and that means we don't have to include the public in every decision.

But every new project, initiative, and decision presents new reasons to ask how much influence over local decisions people should have in a representative democracy. It's true that we elect local officials to make decisions on our behalf. But most community members don't want to vote away their ability to influence *all* future decisions. Likewise, just because elected officials ascribe to a certain political platform doesn't mean those officials will also know how community members feel about specific local decisions, such as how to design a playground or where to build affordable housing.

Public engagement provides the space in which to discuss local issues that transcend political platforms and processes. It is also a space for elected officials to hear from the people who didn't vote for them in the first place. Doing that may not be politically expedient in the near-term, but it is a powerful way to build trust in a community in the long-term. Every local decision comes with a unique set of circumstances and a unique opportunity for community influence. That distinction is at the heart of public engagement in local decisions.

OBJECTION #4: WE ALREADY KNOW WHAT THE PUBLIC THINKS

One thing I have learned in my years practicing public engagement is: never assume we know what the public thinks. We don't automatically know the full range of ideas, concerns, and issues that exist within a community. This applies even to those of us who have been working in the same community for a long time. Familiarity with a community can create complacency, build blind spots, and conceal biases that prevent us from recognizing when conditions shift; communities evolve, attitudes change, economies grow and shrink, new issues surface, and new leaders emerge. For these reasons, I am skeptical of anyone who tells me they have their thumb on the pulse of a community unless they can answer affirmatively to the question, "have you asked recently?"

How can we know what the public thinks? The answer is we do not. We *hope* we know. But in my years doing this work, I have watched clients and partners assume they knew what the community thought about a certain topic or decision, only to find out later they were wrong.

A few years ago, I saw this happen to one of my clients who thought he knew how the public felt about a decision. It turned out he was wrong and his failure to ask had major implications for the cost and schedule for the project.

In this case, a town board wanted to redesign a portion of Main Street to reduce the number of vehicle travel lanes, which a traffic study had shown were unnecessary, and devote some of the newly freed up space to a dedicated two-way bike lane. The planners assumed this would be a "slam dunk" with the community because bike lanes are generally popular. Only after presenting draft plans to the community did the planners find out that bike lanes were not popular among residents and business owners along Main Street.

The project sponsors scratched their heads about this. How, they asked, could anyone be opposed to a bike lane? What the planners found out later was that the surrounding neighbors felt that vehicle parking that was critical to the success of their businesses, which were central to the fabric of the community. Further, many residents communicated that they did not feel the bike lane had been designed with them in mind, but rather for a different population; wealthy, white bike commuters who neither lived nor worked in the neighborhood.

As the discussion unfolded, the project sponsors learned of more layers and nuance about the needs and priorities of the community. Many community members expressed concern that the town had historically ignored them, disinvested in their neighborhood, and failed to involve them in decisions or listen to their needs. After years of this kind of disinvestment, neglect, and institutionalized racism, the neighbors felt that a proposal to install a bike lane was further proof that the town did not care about them. "It's not that we are against bike lanes in all cases," they said. "A bike lane isn't at the top of the list. We never asked for this, but it seems like it's the only thing offered because wealthy bike commuters want a better route to downtown."

The project sponsors did not intend to perpetuate the decades of institutionalized racism and economic disparities, and further damage trust between the government and the residents of the neighborhood. But they did exactly that by assuming they knew what community members wanted. They allowed their experiences and biases to influence their decision about whether to engage the public. Everyone has unconscious bias. Everyone has their own world view and experience. This makes it especially important when conducting public engagement to acknowledge that we can't possibly know what a community thinks, even if we have been living and working in it for years. The only way to find out the range of values, beliefs, and needs in a community is to ask.

OBJECTION #5: INVOLVING THE PUBLIC IS LIKE HANDING THE DECISION OVER TO THEM

I have come to understand that one of the biggest fears among planners and decision-makers is that if we ask the public to participate in a decision, we risk losing control of the decision process: that we are essentially handing the entire decision over to the (unqualified) public. We would be letting the "inmates run the prison" and therefore any level of engagement equates to fully empowering the public to decide.

Let's unpack this misconception by following the logic. Let's say decision-makers *wanted* to give the public 100 percent control over a decision. How would they do that? The only way to fully empower the public—to give a decision completely over to the public—is to organize a referendum. And even then, a vote only allows the public to say yes or no to something. Even then, there are still aspects of that decision the public wouldn't be able to control. Handing a decision to the public isn't even possible without considerable effort.

The notion that engaging the public means relinquishing our responsibility, or losing control, comes from a failure to set clear expectations about what we are asking the public to do. It can be confusing for the public when we fail to clearly describe a decision and what aspects of that decision the public can influence. Without guidance and clear expectations, the members of the public are forced to fill in the blanks. If the community thinks it will have more influence over a decision than it actually does, there will be a gap between expectations and reality, setting the stage for dissatisfaction and frustration.

OBJECTION #6: PUBLIC ENGAGEMENT STIRS THE POT

I was an inquisitive child. I asked so many questions my grandmother used to tell me not to "stir the pot." It was her way of telling me I was causing trouble or provoking a situation that would otherwise be calm. When it comes to certain kinds of decisions, especially those we expect will be controversial, some planners and decision-makers believe that engaging the community could similarly agitate a situation that would otherwise be quiet. The belief is that if we approach the public, communicate about the project, and ask community members what they think, the risk is that they would suddenly be concerned about something they were not concerned about before we asked. That our engagement efforts would somehow *cause* the outrage.

Peter M. Sandman, PhD, the author of *Responding to Community Outrage: Strategies for Effective Risk Communication* describes this phenomenon as the desire to "let sleeping dogs lie." The main problem, he says is, first, we shouldn't assume dogs are sleeping just because they "haven't lunged at your throat yet." And even if the dogs *are* sleeping, he asks, would engaging them really cause a level of concern that wouldn't be there if we hadn't communicated with them at all?[5] If community members are not already concerned about a particular project or decision, our efforts to engage are unlikely to wake them up. Engaging a community openly and honestly is not the cause of controversy. If outrage is uncovered, it is likely that it already existed and any efforts to ignore or stonewall will exacerbate that outrage, not tamp it down.

OBJECTION #7: THE PUBLIC HAS "MEETING FATIGUE"

One of the great ironies of my work is that one of the most common objections to doing public engagement I hear from my clients, colleagues, and partners isn't about whether we are doing *enough* engagement. Rather they are worried we are doing *too much* engagement. *What about meeting fatigue?* To be fair, this question usually comes from planners who are involved in multiple initiatives and planning projects happening at the same time. From their perspective, there are many meetings and engagement opportunities occurring simultaneously. It's true that community members might get confused. Perhaps the public may truly be tired of being engaged.

A variation of the "meeting fatigue" objection is a sentiment that community members are apathetic and unresponsive to decision-makers' attempts to engage. That is, until they aren't. Public managers may attempt to engage the community through the course of a decision, only to find that the public seemingly wait to become interested toward the end. But by that point, the public is upset about not being involved earlier—and they blame the agency or decision-makers. This scenario can be frustrating for public managers and policymakers, especially when they make genuine and sustained attempts to engage the community early in the process.

A colleague of mine described to me how this dynamic plays out in many communities. He told me about a decision process in which his office checked all the boxes for engagement; they sent public notices, put ads in the newspaper, and hosted a public meeting. He lamented that members of the community seemed to ignore these offers, instead waiting until the decision was imminent to show up to express dissatisfaction about not being engaged earlier. As he put it, "it's a two-way street."

There are many reasons why a community may see dramatic swings between fatigue/apathy and outrage. Likewise, there are many reasons why members of a community don't respond to a public notice or a request for comment, or an invitation to a public meeting. Members of the public in communities all over the US have explained to me why they don't get involved until it's too late. Most often it is for two reasons: (1) they don't understand how the decision will affect them, and therefore why they should get involved in the first place and (2) they don't understand their level of influence in the decision.

Members of the public rarely get tired of being engaged in important local government decisions that impact their lives. What wears people out is constant, ineffective, and unclear messaging about public engagement. People are wary of being told "we need your input!" only to feel like their input is ignored and their valuable time wasted. What looks like fatigue is frustration, disappointment, and cynicism. It's a reasonable response to "conventional" participation (discussed in Chapter 3). In fact, "fatigued" participants is not the most worrisome issue. Rather, it is that the public will become apathetic and stop participating in local government decisions altogether. Frustration, cynicism, and apathy set in when community members don't understand why decisions matter to them and when their expectations about their level of influence on a decision don't align with their actual influence.

It doesn't help that our expectations are often communicated in vague terms or hidden in a formal public notice. *Give us your input. Provide comment.* Such statements do not help the public understand why a decision is important to them, or what their level of influence is. This confusion about the importance and their role can lead many members of the public to ignore most invitations to engage. While apathy and meeting fatigue cannot always be avoided, the phenomenon can be managed by following the steps in Part 2 of this book.

****

I purposely excluded some of the more malevolent objections I have heard; the kind that stem from dishonesty, corruption, and fraud. Greed is a powerful motivator that often leads decision-makers to behave with secrecy, stonewalling, and potentially authoritarian tendencies. I acknowledge that such forces exist at all levels of government in the US. My goal in this book is not to reform corrupt decision-makers. My goal is to help the thousands of planning practitioners and decision-makers in the US who believe, at some level, that transparency and participation in government decisions is a worthy goal.

Understanding these objections can help you as a practitioner by unearthing the underlying skepticism that could be preventing you from fully exploring the range of public engagement options available to you. You can also return to this chapter when you are faced with objections from your colleagues, bosses, and members of the public. My hope is that this chapter has given you the tools you need to walk with them through their skepticism, hesitation, and fear—and that you can help overcome those forces together.

REFERENCES

[1] Migchelbrink, K. and S. Van de Walle, A Systematic Review of the Literature on Determinants of Public Managers' Attitudes Toward Public Participation. *Local Government Studies*, 2022. **48**(1): pp. 1–22.

[2] Gakhal, J., *America Speaks*. 2019. Participedia.

[3] Migchelbrink, K. and S. Van de Walle, When Will Public Officials Listen? A Vignette Experiment on the Effects of Input Legitimacy on Public Officials' Willingness to Use Public Participation. *Public Administration Review*, 2020. **80**(2): pp. 271–280.

[4] Creighton, J.L., *The Public Participation Handbook: Making Better Decisions Through Citizen Involvement*. Hoboken, NJ. 2005. Jossey-Bass.

[5] Sandman, P., *Responding to Community Outrage: Strategies for Effective Risk Communication*. Falls Church, VA. 1993.

Six

INTRODUCTION

In previous chapters, we learned about all things that can go wrong with public engagement. With all that bad news, it's no wonder so many public managers are skeptical. Let's now take a step back and consider the reasons we should do public engagement. Sure, one major reason to do public engagement is because we must; many decisions are governed by regulatory processes that require a minimum public engagement effort (such as a public hearing). But there is a multitude of other reasons to do public engagement, ranging from the desire to build public support for decisions, to the hope of sustaining public trust in the public decision-making process.

Scholars and researchers have been exploring these benefits for decades. Generally, these researchers describe the benefits of public engagement in two categories. The first category involves the benefit to *individuals* and participants themselves, such as improved dignity, self-esteem, knowledge, self-confidence, self-actualization, better connection to one's values, expression of identity, and better social connections. The second category of benefit can be described as *institutional* (or managerial). Such benefits improve public decisions and increase political legitimacy. Institutions and agencies achieve these benefits by bringing in a wide range of perspectives on a particular problem or decision. It follows that having more people involved in a public decision means more people will likely accept that decision, hence increasing its legitimacy (and the legitimacy of the governmental entity making the decision).[1]

Public engagement is the process through which governments align public decisions with the needs and values of the communities they serve. That alignment is the foundation for achieving all other benefits of

DOI: 10.4324/9781003451174-7

public engagement. First and foremost, among those benefits is gaining acceptance and public support for decisions. In turn, that public support lends legitimacy to public decisions, which makes future decision-making more efficient and cost-effective. Further, research shows that members of the public are more likely to comply with decisions they support, meaning that governments can spend less time and effort seeking compliance through punitive policies and enforcement.

Beyond these highly practical (and seemingly self-serving) benefits, there is a layer of more ephemeral benefits. Public engagement, when done well, can bring benefits to individuals, such as members of the public and the people who work for government agencies. These benefits include increased knowledge, self-confidence, a better understanding of one's own values, deeper social connections, and increased trust in fellow community members. Quality public engagement can also improve morale among agency staff members and decision-makers. Instead of facing angry and outraged members of the public, agency staff can leverage public engagement to improve their interactions with the public, which can create a better and more satisfying work environment. Among the many benefits of public engagement, below are those that I have found to be the most impactful.

1. **Alignment of public policy with community needs and values.** Engaging in dialogue with the public is the best way to understand what community members need and value. When policymakers work with the public, they learn about the public's perceptions and concerns. This, in turn, can help ensure that the policies, programs, and plans are aligned with community values.

2. **Increased public support and legitimacy**. When members of the public understand how decisions will be made and have a say in how policy decisions are made, they are more likely to trust that those public programs and policies align with their own values. When members of the public understand and trust the decision-making process, they are more likely to support the outcomes of that decision-making process. Public support creates legitimacy (and longevity) for public decisions.

3. **Reduced risk of delay (and cost).** A public decision made unilaterally, without the public's involvement can face so much resistance that it gets delayed or scuttled completely. Public engagement, when implemented concurrently, can reduce the likelihood of such delays.

4. **Increased public trust.** Quality public engagement not only facilitates the decision at hand. It can also help decision-makers build trusting

relationships with the public over the longer-term, which can facilitate future decision processes.

5. **Better decisions.** I often tell my clients that community members are a built-in focus group made up of people who really, truly care about how public decisions will impact their lives. By sharing their expertise and lived experience, members of the public can be a critical partner for decision-makers, helping to uncover unconscious biases and faulty assumptions—and develop new solutions that decision-makers previously not considered.

THE VALUE OF PUBLIC TRUST

It is often said that the ability to trust other people is how we sustain our society. Likewise, trust between decision-makers and everyone else is fundamental to the functioning of any organization, government, or society. Research shows that people who trust the government are more likely to follow rules and consent to policies.[2] Similarly, local governments can achieve more and be more effective at providing services when members of the public believe that decision-makers have their interests in mind. Damage to trust is not only inconvenient, it impedes a local government's ability to get things done, to deliver services and adopt policies that need compliance and cooperation in order to be successful.[3] Public trust is one of the most important requirements for effective democratic governance.

Trust is one of the most important prosocial behaviors, the "glue that holds human society together."[4] People who trust others tend to cooperate more with other people. Human societies have formed and lasted based solely on prosocial behaviors like trust, which gives people the ability to work together to solve problems.[4] Research shows that in our modern world, people who trust others tend to have more confidence in political institutions and authorities.[5] While people who don't trust others think that everyone else is out to break the rules or get away with something, people with greater trust tend to follow the rules because they are not suspicious or afraid of getting duped or swindled; they believe others will follow the rules, too. These trusting people tend to be more accepting of the decisions that public authorities make. In general, public authorities like it when people accept their decisions because authorities don't need to over-enforce and coerce people, which can be very expensive and messy.

The prospect of increased trust is one of the major reasons local governments engage the public. Over the course of my career, I have asked clients, partners, and members of the public what they believe are the benefits of public engagement. There was a surprising throughline in what people told me. The sentiment I heard repeatedly was trust. Trust is the glue that keeps government structures and policies functioning.

My colleagues also tell me they believe trust is a two-way street. A poorly run public engagement process can damage trust between the public and decision-makers, especially if members of the public donate their time and input, only to find out later their input was not used. But decision-makers who engage the public in a transparent manner also generate trust among the public. The more decision-makers engage, the more they, themselves, learn to trust the public. And this mutual building of trust can positively benefit a decision-making process in a variety of ways, such as generating support for public decisions. In this way, political authorities are motivated to build trust with the public out of self-interest: they want to sustain and improve the governmental entity or institution they represent.

The idea that people are more likely to accept policies when they have a hand in creating them is supported by research. The Organization for Economic Co-operation and Development (OECD) conducted a survey on trust in government and public institutions across 22 countries. OECD found that public trust in government can create a variety of benefits that make the job of governing easier and more efficient. The logic is that trust in government institutions can "reduce transaction costs" and help ensure compliance with public policy as well as "reinforce democratic institutions and norms."[6]

OECD notes that public trust serves as both an input to governance as well as an output. That is, as an input, public trust can help governments more efficiently enact policies and gain compliance with those policies. As an output, trust is "an expression of how people perceive their public institutions and what they expect of their government."[6] In that sense, public trust is circular and mutually reinforcing. Governing can be more effective and responsive when people trust their government—because when people trust, they are more likely to support and comply with government policies without coercion. But government needs to be more effective and responsive to generate that public trust in the first place.

WHAT CAN RESEARCH ON TAX MORALE TELL US ABOUT THE BENEFITS OF PUBLIC ENGAGEMENT?

It is hard to identify and measure the benefits of public engagement perhaps in the same way it is hard to measure democracy, or love, or art, or happiness. Many researchers in the field have concluded that empirical research on the benefits and outcomes of public engagement is lagging behind theory.[1,7–13] This book will not fill the gaps in the research. But I can share my professional experiences as well as insight on some of the most illuminating research.

The importance of public trust at all levels of government is clearly important enough that many organizations measure it, track it, and report on it. How does public engagement improve public trust? To explore the effects of public engagement on public trust, let's zoom in on an area of government policy many of us take for granted: taxation.

While many planners are not directly involved in solving the issue of tax compliance and tax evasion in their communities, we can learn a lot from research on tax compliance to better understand how public engagement can improve government decisions. In the world of taxation, actual support for policies is measured by compliance (as opposed what people say); do people pay their taxes or not? And if we agree that compliance with government policies is an expression of some level of public support and trust, then the research on tax compliance can provide a small window into the relationship between public engagement and public trust.

"Tax morale" is a term used to describe people's willingness to pay taxes.[14] Tax morale is the subject of extensive research in the public policy field and can tell us a lot about how public engagement can be deployed in city planning, as well as other areas of local government decision-making. If this seems like a stretch and the thought of reading another word about tax compliance makes your eyes glaze over, stick with me.

When I think of the ways that governments try to encourage people to pay their taxes, I think of enforcement techniques (the stick) or attempts to improve customer-service efficiency (the carrot). But I was fascinated to learn that numerous studies showed that public engagement can also have a significant impact on how people perceive taxes and, more importantly, whether they are willing to pay said taxes.

Evidence suggests that public engagement may be as effective, or even more effective at curbing tax evasion than traditional deterrence measures, such as fines and controls.[15] For example, one study completed by the World Bank Group in 2019 found that municipal governments in Brazil that adopted participatory processes collected much higher levels of locally generated taxes (39 percent more) than other, similar municipalities that did not use participatory processes.[16] Another study with 65,000 participants across 50 countries showed the effects of "bottom up" public engagement on tax compliance, ultimately showing that people are more likely to pay their taxes when they have the chance to share their opinions about how the government spends money[14]. An Austrian study found that participants who were given the chance to make item-by-item decisions on which taxes to pay had higher total tax compliance than people assigned to just pay all taxes lumped together.[17]

What we can learn about the benefits of public engagement from employees who participate in company decisions

The notion that public engagement can generate support for decisions is not limited to government entities. Researchers have also explored engagement in the workplace. Studies show that employee participation in company decisions can bring higher productivity. One study showed that *how* a new company policy or system was implemented mattered more than the specifics of that system. For instance, adopting a "total quality management" system itself did not raise productivity. Rather, allowing for greater employee participation in the decision-making mattered more. Companies that promote joint decision-making with employees have documented higher productivity than other, similar companies.[18] Another study found that when employees were involved in developing performance metrics, employees performed better and managers perceived those metrics to be of better quality and used them more for evaluating and rewarding employees.[19]

People are more willing to pay taxes when they have a say in how those dollars will be spent. These findings are especially powerful because they suggest that giving the public a say in a decision process builds buy-in, not just in a touchy-feely way, but in concrete terms. For many planners and policymakers who deal in relatively abstract terms, of community "visions" and "goals" and "strategies," this research provides an important window into the real-life benefits of public engagement.

It may be too difficult to find an analogous measure of compliance when it comes to community visions and long-range plans. But the research on tax morale suggests that we can apply its conclusions to planning decisions and other areas of policymaking; public engagement can generate more public trust and support of public policies.

QUALITY IS THE KEY TO REALIZING THE BENEFITS OF PUBLIC ENGAGEMENT

We know that public engagement can lead to greater compliance with laws and support of public decisions. But that still leaves big questions about how exactly that happens. What kind of public engagement creates the most support?

It turns out research shows that the benefits of public engagement depend a lot on the quality of the engagement. For insight into the benefits of quality public engagement, we can turn to research conducted by Kathleen Halvorsen, a researcher at Michigan Technological University, which shed light on the real-life impacts of quality public engagement. In this case, those impacts were on the US Forest Service, a federal agency that had experienced decades of dwindling public trust.

In the 1970s and 1980s, the US Department of Agriculture Forest Service (USFS) began to experience a loss of public trust. The publication of Rachel Carson's book *Silent Spring* in 1962 brought a new environmental awareness to American society. The agency had experienced strong public support for its focus on timber production in the 1950s. But by the 1970s, shifting public opinion and the enduring environmental movement began to challenge the agency's policies and practices, particularly clearcutting forests. By the 1980s, environmental activists were pitted against the timber industry, culminating in the now famous conflict over the Northern Spotted Owl. After decades of conflict, lawsuits, and withering public support it was found that by the 1990s, employee morale at the agency was at an all-time low.

Halvorsen's theory was that high-quality public engagement could begin to solve these problems by positively transforming the public's opinions of the agency.[13] In her experiment, Halvorsen worked with USFS representatives to host two kinds of high-quality public engagement activities. Halvorsen defined high-quality participation as activities that were considered comfortable, satisfying, deliberative, and accessible to participants.[13]

The two activities tested in the experiment were "focused conversations" with established community groups and "community dinners" that were open to the general public. The focused conversations took the form of 45-minute interviews conducted with groups such as natural resource advocates and hunting groups, Kiwanis, and women's groups. The dinners were structured so that attendees sat at tables in small groups. A USFS representative was seated at each table and someone at the table was appointed to facilitate while another was selected to take notes. Over the course of the dinner, groups of participants at each table answered a series of questions. At the end of the dinner, each table presented their answers to the larger group.

Participants were surveyed at the end of the project and it was found that participants who felt the meetings were high quality were significantly more likely to believe the USFS was a responsive agency. Astonishingly, after decades of eroded public trust, Halverson reports that, "Just one meeting spent discussing their hopes and fears with agency employees in a comfortable, convenient, and satisfying setting was enough to make them significantly more likely to believe [the agency] was responsive."[13] Halvorsen's experiment shows that public engagement can provide benefits to an agency or municipal entity by leading people to see the agency as being more responsive. The important distinction here is that the participatory activities must have certain high-quality characteristics.

According to Halvorsen, quality public engagement must be satisfying, accessible, and deliberative. Feelings of satisfaction can vary widely among participants. For some people, having a chance to learn from others and communicate with neighbors is satisfying. For many participants, interactive dialogue (in-person or virtual) is more satisfying than one-way techniques such as providing comment at a public hearing or filling out comment cards. Of course, trusting that their feedback will influence the decision is a major contributor to satisfaction. Accessibility, according to Halvorsen, is important to ensure representation and fairness in the engagement process. Accessibility means that meetings are held at convenient times, in locations that are easy to find, accessible by transit and other means, that there is childcare and food provided. Finally, a deliberative process is characterized by an open, respectful, and thorough discussion that includes careful listening and acknowledgment of different viewpoints and values, even if they conflict.[13]

KEY TAKEAWAYS

1. There are many beneficial reasons to conduct public engagement, including benefits to *institutions* (such as gaining acceptance of public decisions) and benefits to *individuals* (such as a better understanding of one's own values).

2. The five most impactful benefits of public engagement are:

- Alignment of public policy and community needs and values
- Increased public support and legitimacy of decisions
- Reduced risk of delay
- Increased public trust
- Better decisions

3. Quality public engagement is the key to realizing the benefits of
   public engagement. Quality can be defined in many ways and generally means that the engagement program is comfortable, satisfying,
   deliberative, and accessible to participants.

REFERENCES

[1] Burton, P., Conceptual, Theoretical and Practical Issues in Measuring the Benefits of Public Participation. *Evaluation*, 2009. **15**(3): pp. 263–284.

[2] Dincecco, M., *State Capacity and Economic Development: Present and Past*. 2017. Cambridge: Cambridge University Press.

[3] Dann, C., *Does Public Trust in Government Matter for Effective Policy-Making?* 2022. Economics Observatory, Bristol, UK.

[4] Schneier, B., *Liars and Outliers Enabling the Trust that Society Needs to Thrive*. 1st ed. 2012. Indianapolis: Wiley.

[5] Brehm, J. and W. Rahn, Individual-Level Evidence for the Causes and Consequences of Social Capital. *American Journal of Political Science*, 1997. **41**(3): pp. 999–1023.

[6] Organization for Economic Co-operation and Development, *Building Trust to Reinforce Democracy*. Paris, France. 2022.

[7] Johnson, C., H.J. Carlson, and S. Reynolds, Testing the Participation Hypothesis: Evidence from Participatory Budgeting. *Political Behavior*, 2023. **45**(1): pp. 3–32.

[8] Shybalkina, I., Toward a Positive Theory of Public Participation in Government: Variations in New York City's Participatory Budgeting. *Public Administration (London)*, 2022. **100**(4): pp. 841–858.

[9] Uddin, K. and B.M. Alam, *Public Participation Process in Urban Planning: Evaluation Approaches of Fairness and Effectiveness Criteria of Planning Advisory Committees*. Routledge Studies in Urbanism and the City. 2021, Milton: Taylor and Francis.

[10] Carpini, M.X.D., F.L. Cook, and L.R. Jacobs, Public Deliberation, Discursive Participation, and Citizen Engagement: A Review of the Empirical Literature. *Annual Review of Political Science*, 2004. **7**(1): pp. 315–344.

[11] Migchelbrink, K. and S. Van de Walle, A Systematic Review of the Literature on Determinants of Public Managers' Attitudes Toward Public Participation. *Local Goverment Studies*, 2022. **48**(1): pp. 1–22.

[12] Gaventa, J. and G. Barrett, Mapping the Outcomes of Citizen Engagement. *World Development*, 2012. **40**(12): pp. 2399–2410.

[13] Halvorsen, K.E., Assessing the Effects of Public Participation. *Public Administration Review*, 2003. **63**(5): pp. 535–543.

[14] Sjoberg, F.M.a.M., Jonathan and Peixoto, Tiago Carneiro and Hemker, Johannes Zacharias and Tsai, Lily Lee, *Voice and Punishment: A Global Survey Experiment on Tax Morale* (World Bank Policy Research Working Paper, 2019. No. 8855.

[15] Torgler, B., Tax Morale and Direct Democracy. *European Journal of Political Economy*, 2005. **21**(2): pp. 525–531.

[16] Touchton, M., B. Wampler, and T. Peixoto, Of Democratic Governance and Revenue: Participatory Institutions and Tax Generation in Brazil. *Governance (Oxford)*, 2019. **34**(4): pp. 1193–1212.

[17] Casal, S., et al., Tax Compliance Depends on Voice of Taxpayers. *Journal of Economic Psychology*, 2016. **56**: pp. 141–150.

[18] Black, S.E. and L.M. Lynch, How to Compete: The Impact of Workplace Practices and Information Technology on Productivity. *The Review of Economics and Statistics*, 2001. **83**(3): pp. 434–445.

[19] Groen, B.A.C., M.J.F. Wouters, and C.P.M. Wilderom, Employee Participation, Performance Metrics, and Job Performance: A Survey Study Based on Self-Determination Theory. *Management Accounting Research*, 2017. **36**: pp. 51–66.

Part Two

Seven

INTRODUCTION

For some, a public decision-making process can seem tedious and bureaucratic. But for many planners and policymakers, a public decision-making process is a dynamic emotional journey into the unknown, filled with complexity. The journey begins the minute we identify a problem that needs a solution; a decision needs to be made. Soon after that, many of us are gripped with another realization: we need to engage the public. My clients describe this as the moment of panic. The reality that we need to engage the public is often accompanied by uncertainty, maybe even fear and panic. In Part 1 of this book, we explored that first part of the journey. Let's call it the descent, in which uncertainties, misconceptions, and mistakes paralyze well-meaning policymakers, causing intense skepticism about public engagement. I assure you it is perfectly normal to feel anxious and overwhelmed by the prospect of engaging the public. And besides, that is only half of the story.

Let's us turn to the other half of the journey, the ascent. That is, how do we translate our fears and anxiety into something practical and operational? The methods outlined in the next few chapters are based on my experiences as a practitioner and what I have learned through the years. To supplement my own experiences, I have conducted research, explored academic literature on the public engagement, and interviewed colleagues, leaders in the field, and everyday members of the public.

I have not invented any of these ideas. Far from it. What I have learned is that public engagement is a field populated by some of the most collaborative and curious professionals in the US, including people in local government administration, public health, planning environmental stewardship, transportation, and climate policy. Likewise, the field of public engagement involves a constantly evolving dialogue where there are no right answers, but rather new perspectives, reflections, and contributions.

DOI: 10.4324/9781003451174-9

Every practitioner of public engagement brings their own unique perspective. What you will see in the pages that follow stems from mine.

These rules and the following chapters are designed to help you and your colleagues jump into the public engagement process quickly. As we established in the beginning of this book, you don't need to be a professional facilitator to apply these methods. You do not need a team of dozens of people, or expensive consultants, or a huge budget. What you do need is an open mind, a willingness to accept uncertainty, and recognition that none of us can control an outcome. We must instead rely on a solid process. A successful public engagement process involves methodical preparation and careful alignment with the technical steps in a decision, which I discuss in detail in Chapters 9 and 10. If applied throughout your work, these three rules will bring ease to your public engagement process. The detailed steps and methods outlined in the remaining chapters of this book are grounded in three simple rules. Think of these rules as your foundation. Everything else builds from here.

RULE #1: ENGAGE EARLY

The success of your public engagement process depends on what you do *before* the public decision is made. You have heard this refrain repeated in various ways throughout this book because I believe it is one of the most fundamental principles of public engagement. In Chapter 4, we learned all about the dynamics of engaging late and how damaging that can be for decision-makers and the public. The flip side of that is early engagement. If you take one thing away from this book, it is this simple principle: engage the community as early in a decision process as you possibly can. Adhering to this principle alone will bring greater ease to any public engagement program you lead. Not only is early engagement better for the overall engagement process, research shows that both decision-makers and participants prefer to engage early in the decision process than have to wait until late in the process.[1] By then, everyone's ability to influence the decision has declined significantly.

Here are just a few of the many reasons to engage early:

- **Uncover your community's issues and concerns *before* making a decision.** The biggest benefit of engaging early is that you give yourself a chance to understand the community's perceptions, feelings, needs, concerns, and ideas before you have reached key milestones in your project that would be expensive to change or reverse. One of the most painful experiences in public decision-making is being forced into an expensive course-correct that comes in the wake of public protest or legal appeal. When you take the time to understand how community members feel about a project early in the decision process, you build yourself a cushion and additional time to address the community's concerns. In this way, you can reduce the chances of being surprised at a public hearing, when it can be too late to make substantive changes to your project without causing significant delay and expense.

- **Engaging early helps you build trust with community members**. As we learned in Chapter 6, trust is one of the most important inputs and outputs of public engagement. By bringing members of the community into the decision process long before a decision is made, you are signaling your intent to design a transparent process, listen to the community's ideas, and ultimately share influence. This is the foundation of trust. The beginning of a decision process is the ideal time to communicate to the public some key pieces of information, such as how you intend to make the decision, what the timeline is, what aspects of the decision can be influenced by the community, and how community members can be involved throughout the process. When community members become involved in a public decision from the very beginning, they have an opportunity to trust that decisions won't be made without their input—or at least without their knowledge. Engaging early helps you combat the sentiment that the final decision "was a done deal" by demonstrating that the decision process will include members of the public at every stage, not just the very end.
- Engaging early helps you **build a culture of collaboration with the community** by engaging throughout the decision process, especially at the beginning when key decision factors are still being developed, such as defining the problem to be solved, brainstorming options for solving the problem, and selecting the criteria to evaluate the solution.

So many of the problems we experience with hostile public meetings, "difficult" people, scuttled projects, bad press, expense, and delay could be prevented or mediated through early engagement. Imagine heading into a public hearing with the knowledge that you had already taken the time to uncover key issues, addressed the concerns you could, and in cases where you couldn't, explained why. Engaging early will not only improve relationships with community members and help build better public decisions, but it will also make your public engagement process much easier on you and your team.

RULE #2: STRIVE FOR TRANSPARENCY

A transparent decision is one in which the community has an opportunity to understand the decision-making process and the criteria used to make that decision. Creating transparency means disclosing all key information and context about a potential decision. It also means disclosing the intentions, motivations, and biases of the decision-makers. Without transparency, community members struggle to understand why decisions are made and how those decisions will impact their lives. This can lead to frustration, mistrust, and even protest.

Although there are insincere reasons decision-makers fail to be transparent in their decisions (such as corruption), my experience with clients and partners is that decision-makers often resist transparency for more innocent reasons. These reasons include fear of being seen as incompetent, a misdirected sense of responsibility (i.e. "the public elected us to make this decision"), concern about losing control of the decision process, or plain old disorganization. The catch is that the public doesn't care why a decision lacks transparency. They don't care why decision-makers meet behind closed doors or fail to provide necessary background information. Such opacity always looks nefarious from the outside and can have negative consequences for public decisions.

There are many benefits of transparency. Involvement of an informed public can improve the quality of decisions, increase accountability, and reduce corruption. I'm not surprised that transparency is a buzzword in today's world of public engagement. Policymakers talk a lot about how important transparency is and how wonderful it would be to have transparent decisions. But there is not a lot of guidance on what exactly makes a decision transparent.

How do we actually *do* transparency?

To help you better understand the mechanics of transparency, the sections below include a list of concrete ways that you can increase transparency in your decision-making processes.

How to increase transparency in public decision-making

1. **Communicate what the decision is, who will make the decision, and by when.** To enhance transparency, it is important to communicate the right kind of information about the decision at hand—and

at the right time. Often, decision-makers communicate unnecessary information about a project to appear transparent. For instance, sometimes you'll see an announcement about a public meeting that describes, in detail, a long list of tasks in the scope or work. Sometimes a project description will say how the project was funded, or what the overall vision is, or what the desired outcomes will be. These are important pieces of information. But they do not convey transparency. When transparency is your aim, there are three things that are most important to communicate about a decision: (1) *What is the decision that will be made*, (2) *Who will make the decision*, and (3) *When that decision will be made*. A fourth important piece of information that communicates transparency is (4) *How the public can influence the decision*. Answers to these questions are the essence of transparency. (Chapter 9 provides a proven way to answer these questions with your team.)

2. **Disclose the steps that will be made to make the decision.** Virtually all public decisions include a series of steps that are followed to come to a final decision. These steps are usually a variation of the following: (1) define a need, (2) define the scope, (3) explore the existing situation, (4) create solutions, (5) evaluate solutions, and (6) decide. Some decision-makers communicate these steps to the public and others do not. Each one of these steps represents an important milestone, which you can also think of as a mini decision. As you make each mini decision, it becomes more expensive and time consuming to reverse course. Even if you and your team have the best intentions and are following a rational decision model, you can still inadvertently neglect the task of communicating the steps in your decision process to the public. The less the public knows about each mini decision, the more a final decision will appear to be shrouded in secrecy. If you don't communicate milestones clearly, the public won't know you're following a defined process. It will appear to the public as though you did not arrive at the final decision in a rational or fair manner. Or worse, it could appear as though you arrived at a final decision in a dishonest or unethical way. Absent information about how a decision is being made, members of the public are left to fill in the blanks. The decision could appear to be "a done deal," the result of incompetence, or worse, the product of corruption. Instead, you can increase transparency by communicating the steps of the decision process and then deploying continuous communication throughout the process to explain where you are along those steps at any given point in time.

3. **Clearly explain what aspects of the decision the public can influence.** As I described above, all public decisions involve a series of milestones, or mini decisions. For example, consider a project to redesign a streetscape along a mixed-use corridor. There are hundreds of decisions to be made about how the street will look and function. Many of these decisions are highly technical and regulated (such as the radius of the curbs, or the brightness of the bulbs in the streetlights). Those are not aspects of a decision the public can influence. But other aspects of the decision *can* be influenced by the public, such as the location and design of street furniture. These are aspects of a decision that can be open to interpretation—and input. Some aspects of the decision fall in the middle. One design item that is often mistaken as a given is the location of a mid-block pedestrian crossing. Engineers will tell you that is a highly technical decision based on warrants and a variety of other factors. Certain aspects of that decision do depend on technical and legal requirements. But the decision of where to put a mid-block pedestrian crossing must also consider detailed and nuanced observations of human behavior. We can expedite our understanding of these things by incorporating the lived experience of those who use the corridor daily. The real challenge is to figure out what aspects of the decision the public can influence and which aspects the public cannot. (Chapter 9 describes how to identify which aspects of a decision can and cannot be influenced by the public.)

4. **Apologize for past mistakes and failures you or your predecessors made when involving (or not involving) community.** In his book about risk communications, Peter Sandman laments, "American society is very forgiving of the repentant sinner, but not of the unrepentant sinner."[2] Apologizing for mistakes and misbehavior is a powerful and necessary way to build trust and accountability with members of a community. How does that work? Admitting when we have made mistakes can enhance transparency by shining a light on our own actions and acknowledging that we didn't get it right. Many decision-makers dislike admitting mistakes or apologizing, especially when they believe they did nothing wrong. Perhaps the apology was for something their predecessors did or for something that was truly an accident. But compare this to knocking over a lamp at a friend's house. Even if it was an accident, we still offer

an apology. It is also important to express an authentic apology. Sandman describes the example of the Exxon Valdez spill in 1989, one of the largest oil spills in US history. He notes that the company did irreparable harm to its own reputation because it was unable to apologize quickly or effectively. When Exxon did finally apologize, it placed ads in newspapers, but the message came across as a weak non-apology in the vein of, "A terrible thing happened to Exxon in Prince William Sound."[2] The effect of no apology or an inauthentic apology like this is to communicate one's unwillingness to be open about what *really* happened. Unwillingness to talk about what really happened looks a lot like stonewalling, which is the opposite of transparency. Apologies go a long way toward establishing trust and making future decision processes easier.

5. **Demonstrate your openness to hearing all perspectives.** The best way to demonstrate your openness is this: listen. Listen instead of refuting, rebutting, or piling on. Listening is simple, but not always easy. Many policymakers feel they need to have a response to questions before anyone asks. We feel compelled to refute any comments that we believe would contradict, confuse, or derail a decision. Maybe we just want to "educate" the public, believing they will naturally come to the same conclusion we did about a desired course of action. Or maybe we want to control the dialogue at all times for fear that things may turn negative or that disinformation will proliferate. Listening without refuting is one of the hardest skills to master. But it is one of the most important skills for a policymaker to have. In Chapter 10, I offer techniques that can make listening a little bit easier.

6. **Acknowledge the challenges you expect to face during the decision process.** This one is simple: admit what you don't know. An example of this would be, "We know there is a congestion issue at this intersection, but we don't yet know how to solve it. That is why we are pursuing this project." Or maybe "We don't yet know how we will fund this project, but we are doing everything we can to figure it out." Rather than seeing you as incompetent, members of the public find it refreshing to hear decision-makers admit they don't know the answer. Acknowledging the challenges you face as a policymaker (along with a transparent plan to overcome those challenges) sends a strong signal to the public that the decision is not "a done deal."

7. **Make sure all necessary information is accessible to the community.** This is arguably the most straightforward way to ensure transparency. Providing basic information is an administrative task. But policymakers often fail to provide the most basic information about a project out of fear that we are sharing too much or for fear of what the public will do with the information. Other times we fail to share this information because we are too busy to update our website, or because we have an inefficient communication system. Most of the information we fail to share is actually public information, anyway. And rather than make the public jump through hoops to get it, why not just provide it? Put it on the website. Send it around to the email list. Use whatever tool allows you to disseminate information in the most efficient manner. It's always a good idea to err on the side of sharing more information rather than less. But if your capacity is limited, focus on providing the most important pieces of information that communicate transparency (which are details about what the decision is, who is making it, and when). To enhance transparency even more, you can make other information available such as the dates and locations of past and future meetings, notes from all past meetings, maps and drafts of design documents, background reports, a sign-up form for those who want to be included on a mailing list, a schedule, and contact information for those who have questions.

8. **Communicate information about how the decision/project is funded and any potential conflicts of interest.** Declaring conflicts of interest is a foundation of ethics in public decision-making. This can become even more important for smaller communities, where leaders and decision-makers wear many hats. It is not unusual for the mayor of a village to be a business owner, or a town board member to also be a major property owner. In these contexts, it is more important than ever to declare a potential conflict of interest, even if it is only a perceived conflict. Like apologizing, the willingness to acknowledge that you may have a personal or financial interest in a project (even if that interest is ceremonial or no more than a perceived interest) signals your openness to sharing what is really going on.

9. **Communicate how the community's input was used in a decision.** If you have diligently provided information to the public throughout a decision process, such as notes from meetings and

workshops, drafts, and background information, it should be relatively straightforward to demonstrate to the public how input was used. It's as simple as saying, *"Here is what we heard from the public and here is what we did."* For example, let's say as part of a street redesign project, community members asked for on-street parking and a ten-foot-wide cycle track for the length of the corridor. During the design process, you found that the narrow width of the street, the placement of existing buildings, and the location of curbs made a ten-foot-wide cycle track infeasible. Instead, the engineers found a way to fit a regular bike lane between the on-street parking and the curb. This solution, including how it came about, is a key piece of information to communicate to the public. In this case, don't assume the public will see the virtue of your design process. You need to make that connection explicit. For instance, *"We heard overwhelmingly that the community wanted a cycle track and so we committed to finding a solution. Given the physical constraints of the corridor the closest solution to achieve that goal was a protected bike lane."* That simple analysis demonstrates to people that you're willing to share what their neighbors and friends had to say about the project, even if it was not convenient, and even if community members asked for things you can't or won't do. Even if you have to say no or present a compromise. This is a critical step in proving to the community that you have a responsive process, and that you are accountable for responding to what the public said.

10. **Communicate how the community's input was not used in a decision, and why.** One of my teachers and mentors has a saying about this concept: "If not, why not?" In other words, if you can't do something the public asked you do to, you should be able to explain why not. And if you can't explain why not, then you may need to reconsider that aspect of the decision. I have been part of many projects in which decision-makers failed to explain why they couldn't do things the public wanted. Those were lost opportunities to demonstrate transparency. In many cases, there are reasonable explanations for why the public's requests cannot be accommodated. Even saying "no" presents an opportunity to show you listened by describing how you considered the public's request very carefully. Sometimes, something completely unexpected happens: just asking the question "why not" as a design team creates a breakthrough. Everyone looks at each other and realizes there is no good reason why not. So that

"no" becomes a "yes." That is an opportunity to increase transparency by telling the public how you listened.

If you felt a little uncomfortable as you read this list, you're not alone. Establishing a transparent decision process can seem scary or counter-intuitive to many local leaders and decision-makers. There is a reason they say no one wants to see how the sausage is made. Opening a decision process in this way can feel messy and disorganized, as though we are abdicating our responsibility or losing control. Many of my colleagues believe they should resolve problems and work out the kinks before presenting something to the public. Others feel that if they give an inch, the public will take a mile. As decision-makers you may feel you were elected or appointed or hired to your position because it is your job to gather the facts, evaluate options, and make a recommendation. In that sense transparency can feel like potential irrelevance, perceived incompetence, or weakness. Transparency is none of those things. True competence, strength, and leadership is having the gumption to stand in front of a crowd of community members and say "I don't know. But let's solve this together."

RULE #3: RESPECT THE PUBLIC

When we think of unruly public meetings, the image that comes to mind is often that of the angry crowd and people yelling insults at decision-makers and their staff. Over the course of my career, I have witnessed a lot of disrespectful behavior. Oddly, much of the disrespectful behavior I have seen didn't come from the public. It came from decision-makers and their representatives.

A few years ago, I was staffing a public meeting that I had helped organize and facilitate. We organized the meeting to introduce the project to the community and ask for feedback on a handful of potential solutions for a safety issue along a key corridor in a small city. Toward the end of the meeting, after formal activities concluded, participants began to filter out of the room and some lingered to ask questions or connect with neighbors. A small group of staff had gathered around one of the full-size maps displayed on a large table, provided so that participants could write comments or questions directly. I could hear them laughing as I approached. I realized they were reading aloud some of the comments provided by members of the public and ridiculing them for the supposed lunacy of their ideas, their ignorance, or lack of understanding.

I do not share this example to shame anyone who has participated in this kind of venting or blowing off steam at the end of a big public meeting. Many of us have done this. I share this to demonstrate how easy it is to behave disrespectfully toward the public. In fact, it's so common there are TV shows devoted to it. As planners and decision-makers, we have been disrespecting the public for decades. In fact, the term NIMBY (Not in My Back Yard) has been around since at least the 1980s, and possibly much longer than that.[3] NIMBY is a pejorative term that has a history of being used by decision-makers, planners, developers, and applicants of various sorts to describe people who oppose a development or project in their community. It is believed that the term was originally coined to describe groups opposing hazardous waste operations, affordable housing, and social service facilities, such as group homes.[4] In today's context, the term is often understood to describe opposition groups believed to be motivated by racial segregation and class inequality. In my experience, it is a term used in all the above cases—and also simply to describe any individual or group that comes to the table with questions and ideas that are contrary to the opinions of those in power. The term implies that it is somehow selfish and irrational to question a public proposal at all. Taking the public's concerns seriously is not "giving in." It is being respectful and transparent.[2]

Variations of the term NIMBY have emerged over the years, as well. Some notable versions include BANANA (build absolutely nothing any-where near anything), NOPE (not on planet earth), PIITBY (put it in their backyard), and WIIFM (what's in it for me?). There are also terms to describe the opposite, including YIMBY (yes in my backyard) and KIIMBY (keep it in my backyard).[5] Policymakers use these terms to disregard those who oppose a decision (or in some cases, those who support a decision). It is an accepted way to disrespect the public when we don't agree. We are quick to call people YIMBYs or NIMBYs and it allows us to shut our ears and disregard people's lived experiences. It is an excuse to approach the public without empathy.[6]

Considering how easy it is to fall into the NIMBY-hating trap, it is important to remember that our responsibility as planners and policymakers is to respect the public by respecting all perspectives. This includes perspectives we don't agree with; perspectives and ideas we think are unreasonable, uninformed, or ignorant. Just because planners have an educational credential or are in a position of authority does not mean we are all-knowing. We do not know everything about the lived experience of everyone who participates in a public decision.

Consider preconceptions we bring, as planners and decision-makers, to any public decision. We use these preconceptions subtly, and not so subtly, to discount perspectives brought by members of the public. We may write off people's opinions if those people don't have planning or architecture credentials. But we may also discount people's opinions, even if they do have those credentials, simply because we subconsciously assign an agenda or a persona to that person.

Peter Sandman also describes the dynamics of disrespecting of the public and the damaging effects that can have on public trust and credibility. According to Sandman, the majority of the public fall into a category he calls "interested and alert," meaning that while they are interested in a decision, they are not highly involved. They are not part of the small, but vocal opposition. They are not part of any activist group, nor are they considered a NIMBY. Not yet, anyway. But this interested and alert majority is watching the way we treat the so-called NIMBYs and activists. If we are disrespectful and contemptuous of the activists, others will see this. The activists will become "the public's protectors."[2] When that happens, the interested and alert majority are more likely to join the activists, making future public engagement much harder for everyone. On the other hand, if we treat NIMBYs with respect while they continue fighting, they risk being viewed as unreasonable by everyone else. Ultimately the NIMBYs risk being marginalized by the less outraged majority.

There is one important exception to this: Showing respect for the public does not mean we ever allow members of the public to display behavior that is disruptive, discriminatory, or violent in any way. Respectful behavior goes two ways. It is important for decision-makers to establish clear ground rules and set boundaries for what is considered respectful conduct, especially at public meetings or any time we invite members of the public to interact with each other—whether that is in-person or virtual. See Appendix A for sample public meeting ground rules and a safety checklist for public meetings.

KEY TAKEAWAYS

Public engagement can seem like a complicated and scary endeavor. I have found that it is helpful to keep focused on a few essential principles (or "rules") to stay focused and grounded throughout the process. Check in with theses rule at various stages throughout the decision-making process to make sure you haven't lost track of them. To recap, those rules are:

1. **Engage early** to uncover the community's perceptions, concerns, and ideas before you make decisions. Build with community members by bringing them into the process long before a decision is made and help build a culture of collaboration in your community.
2. **Strive for transparency** to ensure the community has an opportunity to understand the decision-making process and criteria used to make a decision. The ten methods presented in this chapter will help increase transparency and help avoid frustration, mistrust, and even outrage among the public.
3. **Respect the public,** including activists and NIMBYs. Remember, the interested and alert majority are watching to see how you treat the NIMBYs. If you are disrespectful and combative with the NIMBYs, they can position themselves as protectors of the public, which can push the interested and alert majority over into the outraged category.

REFERENCES

[1] Migchelbrink, K. and S. Van de Walle, A Systematic Review of the Literature on Determinants of Public Managers' Attitudes Toward Public Participation. *Local Government Studies*, 2022. **48**(1): pp. 1–22.

[2] Sandman, P., *Responding to Community Outrage: Strategies for Effective Risk Communication.* American Industrial Hygiene Association; 1st edition (June 1, 1993), Falls Church, VA 1993.

[3] Borell, K. and Å. Westermark, Siting of Human Services Facilities and the Not in My Back Yard Phenomenon: A Critical Research Review. *Community Development Journal*, 2016. **53**(2): pp. 246–262.

[4] Gerrard, M., The Victims of Nimby. *Fordham Urban Law Journal*, 1994. **21**: p. 495.

[5] Stephens, R.B., *Plannerese Dictionary*. 1994. Urban and Regional Planning, College of Environmental Design, California State Polytechnic University, San Luis Obispo, CA.

[6] Gregory, R., *Structured Decision Making a Practical Guide to Environmental Management Choices*, R. Gregory, Editor. 2012. Chichester, West Sussex: Wiley-Blackwell.

Eight

INTRODUCTION

A few years ago, I was standing in front of a crowd of 95 people, facilitating a public meeting about a plan to restore a flood plain in a residential neighborhood, when one of the participants raised her hand and asked, "Who's making this decision?"

I realized in that moment that I didn't know the answer. I sheepishly looked over to the side of the room, where my clients were lined up in folding chairs along the wall. They were a mix of staff members from different agencies (a federal agency, two state agencies, and two local municipalities). As I looked to them, I could see in their body language; they didn't know, either.

I bumbled through an inadequate answer. It was an embarrassing moment for me as a facilitator. While it seems like the most basic piece of information to clarify before hosting a large public meeting, you might be surprised how often planners and decision-makers do this. We get away with it much of the time because no one thinks to ask the question. But the consequences are still real. Not knowing or communicating a decision can lead to misunderstandings among project sponsors, government entities, and members of the public. It can lead to unclear messaging, ineffective participation, and project delays.

Before we opened the doors to that public meeting, my clients and I thought we were prepared. We knew we had a big a project. We had a scope. We had a very long list of tasks and a very complicated project management Gantt chart. But we did not have a simple explanation of what exactly the decision was, who was making the decision, and by when.

That experience inspired me to revisit one of the most important concepts I learned from the International Association of Public Participation (IAP2), which is that "public participation should be oriented

DOI: 10.4324/9781003451174-10

toward making a decision." Being decision-oriented, according to IAP2 means that we must first define what the decision is before undertaking a public engagement program. In that light, I now advise clients and colleagues to do this one step first before anything else: Define the public decision to be made. This chapter defines what a decision is and how the rational decision-making framework can help us conduct public engagement more easily.

WHAT IS A DECISION?

The Oxford English Dictionary defines a decision as "the action or process of deciding something or of resolving a question."[1] A decision is the process of resolving a question. In our daily lives, we resolve questions constantly. For example, should I eat oatmeal or fruit for breakfast? Should I buy a new car? Should I wear heels or flats? Decision-making is a process by which individuals or groups make choices among different alternatives. It involves identifying and evaluating options based on certain criteria, weighing the pros and cons of each option, and ultimately choosing the option that best aligns with one's goals and values.

Some decision-making models emphasize rational thinking and logical analysis, while others recognize the role of emotions, intuition, and personal biases in shaping decision-making. Time constraints, uncertainty, and complexity can also influence our decisions. Decision-making involves breaking down complex decisions into smaller, more manageable parts, and using analytical methods to evaluate the potential outcomes of each option. The art and science of decision-making is central to any discussion of public engagement because public decisions often involve complex and high-stakes choices with competing interests and priorities. And public decisions can have significant impacts on people's lives.

In the context of local governments and planning, we may also refer to decision-making as "rational policymaking." One way to uncover whether there is, in fact, a decision at hand is to pay close attention to the language you're using to talk about your project. The terms we use are clues: words like "develop," "adopt," "accept," "implement," or "evaluate" are decisional words. In the planning context, a town board would *adopt* a Comprehensive Plan. A planning board would *approve* a development application. When you hear words like this, you'll know there is probably a decision lurking somewhere.

Sometimes the decision is not immediate or obvious. But it is there somewhere. The key may be the timeline. The decision may have already occurred, which means it's in the past (oops). Or the decision is not yet defined, which means it exists at some point in the future. Conducting public engagement for decisions that are in the past or too far off future can be problematic. When there is a mismatch between the timing of a decision and public engagement activities, it's easy to stray away from public engagement and find ourselves doing other things, such as public relations, research, or marketing. (There is nothing inherently wrong with activities like public relations. There is a time and a place for disseminating one-way information. But we confuse public relations with public engagement at our own peril. Public engagement works best when oriented toward a public decision.)

HOW CAN DECISION SCIENCE HELP?

To illustrate how important it is to define your decision before implementing a public engagement program, let us turn briefly to some key lessons from experts in the field of decision-making. One of the amazing things I discovered while writing this book is that there is an entire field of researchers across the globe who study the science of human decision-making. The origin of this science can be traced back to the early 20th century, with the work of scholars such as Frank Ramsey, Leonard Savage, and John von Neumann.[2] These scholars established the foundation for decision theory, which studies uncertainty and how individuals make choices in the face of incomplete information. In the 1950s and 1960s, decision theory began to be applied to business and management problems, giving rise to the field of "decision analysis." Decision analysis involves using quantitative methods to evaluate alternatives and make informed decisions, and it has become an important tool in fields such as operations research, organizational behavior, finance, and strategic management.[3]

Over time, decision science has evolved to include a wide range of disciplines and approaches, including behavioral economics, cognitive psychology, and computer science. Today, decision science is a multidisciplinary field that combines insights from many different specialties to help individuals and organizations make better decisions.

Given the history of decision science, one would think it would be easy to define what a "good" decision is. A good public decision is one that creates a good outcome. Right? Not so fast. The problem with that logic is that it doesn't really help us when we're in the midst of making a decision. We can't measure all the outcomes of a decision while we're making the decision. We probably won't know all the outcomes of our decision for months or years. That's why we can make a good decision and still get a bad outcome, or vice versa.

In their book *Decision Quality: Value Creation from Better Business Decisions*, Carol Spetzler, Hannah Winter, and Jennifer Meyer point out that, "determining the quality of a decision by its outcome would require withholding judgment until everything there is to know about the result becomes available."[4] That clearly isn't practical, especially in the context of local government decisions where there are thousands of variables and factors that influence the outcome of a decision. Instead, they say, the best way to measure the quality of decisions is to evaluate *how* those decisions are made.

So, what makes a good decision *process*? Researchers and authors have developed a multitude of decision frameworks, some of which you may have seen at some point during your career. If you do a quick internet search, you will find that commonly used frameworks for decision-making and rational policymaking generally include five to seven steps. First, a problem must be identified. Second, goals and criteria must be specified. Third, alternatives must be developed. Fourth, the alternatives should be evaluated using the goals and criteria. Finally, the decision should be made that best aligns with your goals. This is a simplified version of the rational decision-making model, but many of the popular models follow a similar structure.

Some examples of rational decision-making frameworks include GOFER (Goals clarification, Options generation, Facts-finding, Effects, and Review) and DECIDE (Define the problem, Establish the criteria, Consider the alternatives, Identify the best alternative, Develop and implement a plan of action, and Evaluate).[5,6] The authors of *Decision Quality* also offer a step-by-step framework (Frame, Alternatives, Information, Values & Trade-offs, Reasoning, Commitment to action). These frameworks may be familiar to public managers and it's likely you may have used a similar process to complete a policy analysis or planning project.

A quality decision, then, is one in which a quality process is used: in which each step is undertaken with care. A decision is only as good as the weakest link in the steps. This is a very process-y way of understanding decision-making. But it's a critical distinction for anyone involved in project management and decision-making, especially in the context of local government decisions.

A typical decision process

The illustration below shows my adaption and consolidation of a variety of the most widely used decision-making models into a six-step process to help illustrate how the typical decision process can align with public engagement. This six-part process includes the following steps:

1. **Identify the problem/scope the decision**. The first step in any decision process involves defining the nature of the problem. For public decisions, it is especially important to define the decision precisely, by describing the decision itself, who will make the decision, and when.

2. **Analyze existing conditions/gather information.** Most public decisions involve some level of information-gathering to help us understand our starting point, what plans or decisions have already been made, and what data are needed to move forward. Planning projects usually require that we understand existing conditions and gather technical information, existing land uses, population and demographics, market trends, traffic patterns, zoning, environmental constraints, and many others.

3. **Develop decision criteria/goals.** This stage of the project is where we decide *how* we want to decide. What measures will we use to generate and evaluate various solutions to our problem? Criteria are an essential component of transparent decision-making because they communicate how a decision will be made based on what is most important to the community and decision-makers.

4. **Generate solutions to the problem.** For this step, you will identify a list of potential solutions for the problem at hand. It is important to find more than one potential solution to the problem to ensure that you don't limit or bias yourself to the first solution that comes to mind. Sometimes practitioners include a "base case" or "do-nothing" option to convey what would happen if none of the potential solutions were selected.

5. **Evaluate solutions.** Evaluation processes can range in complexity depending on the decision at hand. The key is to compare your potential solutions to the decision criteria. Some practitioners use a decision matrix to help facilitate the evaluation process. A matrix helps consider multiple factors across potential solutions to narrow down into one final decision. A decision matrix is also a helpful tool if you need to add weights to certain criteria.

6. **Decide.** Pick the solution.

Typical Decision Process

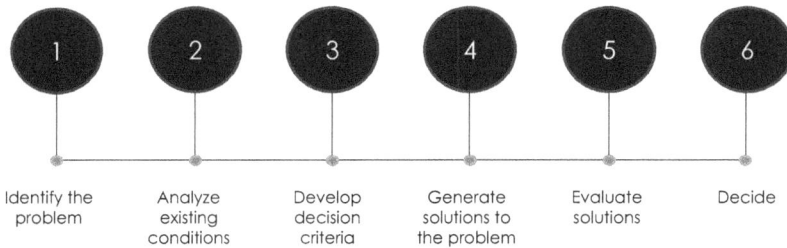

Figure 8.1 A typical decision process.

Planners and policymakers don't need to become decision-scientists to make better public decisions. But we should understand the fundamentals of decision-making. This knowledge and practice can lift public decisions to the next level. You will see in the next few chapters that a systematic decision process is an important foundation for successful public engagement. Making a good decision means following a well-defined process. Likewise, successfully incorporating public engagement into our decision-processes requires that we have an understanding the basic steps in a decision.

REFERENCES

[1] Oxford English Dictionary, in Oxford English Dictionary. 2023, Oxford University Press, Oxford, UK.
[2] Parmigiani, G., Decision Theory Principles and Approaches, ed. L.Y.T. Inoue. 2009. Chichester, West Sussex, UK: John Wiley & Sons.
[3] Howard, R.A., Decision Analysis: Applied Decision Theory. 1966. Stanford Research Institute, Menlo Park, CA.
[4] Spetzler, C.S., Decision Quality Value Creation from Better Business Decisions. 2016. Hoboken, NJ: John Wiley & Sons, Inc.
[5] Harmoni L. Mann & C. Power, The GOFER Course in Decision Making. Teaching Decision Making to Adolescents. J. Baron & R.V. Brown, Editors. Lawrence Erlbaum Associates, Inc., Mahwah, NJ. 1991. pp. 61–78.
[6] Guo, K.L., DECIDE: A Decision-Making Model for More Effective Decision Making by Health Care Managers. Health Care Manag (Frederick), 2020. **39**(3): pp. 133–141.

How decision science makes public engagement easier

Nine

Preparation is the path to easier public engagement.

INTRODUCTION

If your public engagement activities seem ad hoc and disorganized and you want to learn how to make it easier, this chapter is for you. The best way to make engagement easier is through adequate preparation. That preparation can be completed in four steps: (1) define your decision, (2) set engagement objectives, (3) scan the engagement landscape, and (4) write a public engagement plan. If that seems like a lot of work to do before you even get to doing the engagement, you're right. But I'm going to let you in on a secret: these preparation steps are the key to making engagement easier. The collaborative nature of public engagement means that even in the preparation stages, you will be seeking the opinions of your team and the public. And in that way the preparation for public engagement is part of the doing.

As you read this chapter, keep in mind that public engagement is rarely linear. You may need to iterate, circle back, and readjust as you learn new information, or as new challenges present themselves. This can seem challenging to planners and decision-makers because we're often attempting to align a very linear decision process with a non-linear engagement process. That is normal. As you read through the steps on the following pages, keep in mind that throughout any decision process, it may be necessary to reassess, revisit, and revise your public engagement process.

#1: DEFINE YOUR DECISION

As we learned in Chapter 3, an effective public engagement program must have a clearly defined public decision. Here's what a clearly defined decision can contribute to your public engagement process:

- A defined decision helps you and your team agree on the scope of the project, the decision process, and timing.

DOI: 10.4324/9781003451174-11

- A defined decision lays the groundwork for clear messaging to the public.
- A defined decision ensures you and your team better understand how the public can (or can't) influence the decision; and
- A defined decision helps you and your team identify key participants (such as who is most impacted and interested).

The International Association of Public Participation (IAP2) framework suggests that to properly define a decision, we must first identify the who, what, and when of a decision.[1] I have adapted this framework to help my clients and partners define a decision by asking the following three questions:

1. What is the decision?
2. Who will make the decision?
3. When will the decision be made?

Answering these three questions accurately and succinctly can be bigger challenge that it first appears. To illustrate the deceptive simplicity of defining a decision, let's consider two examples. In one example, a town board is considering a development application seeking to construct a community center next to the senior high school. The decision in this case is relatively straightforward: the town board will decide on the night of the public hearing whether to approve the application, deny the application, or approve with conditions. The three components of this decision are relatively simple to communicate. First, the decision is to *approve* or *deny*. Second, the decision will be made by the *town board*. Lastly, the decision will be made the *night of the hearing*, which will happen on a specific date.

Now imagine a slightly different scenario. Let's say you are the staff planner in that same town, only you were appointed eight months ago to manage a feasibility study for a new community center. What is the decision in that case? Is completing a feasibility study a decision? Not exactly. Nor is a feasibility study the same as deciding whether and how and where to build a community center (that would be a future decision). The decision in that moment is related only to the feasibility study itself: whether to accept the report as final and forward the recommendations to the town board for consideration. Whose decision would that be? It might be yours as the planner or administrator. Further, the timing of that decision may be determined by many factors, including the schedule for completing a feasibility study, and the time it takes to find a consultant to do the work.

You can see how these two examples might at first appear to be the same decision. But upon closer inspection, it's clear that they are two different kinds of decisions, distinguished by the nature of the decision, who will make the decision, and by when.

Let's consider a more common, but no less complex scenario. In this, case let's say you are a planner who is appointed to manage a collaborative effort between your town, a neighboring village, the county, the Metropolitan Planning Organization (MPO), and the state Department of Transportation (DOT) to complete a bicycle and pedestrian plan for a two-mile stretch of Main Street. To define the decision, we need to answer what, who, and when. But when we start asking questions like "what is the decision" and "who will make it?" things can get a little murky. Is the plan going to be adopted? Or will it just be accepted? If so, by whom? Perhaps the decision power resides with the village because the village received the grant to pay for the corridor study in the first place. Or maybe it is the state's ultimate decision whether to accept the plan because Main Street is a state road. Many public decisions involve multiple jurisdictions, making it more important than ever to properly define the decision at hand. The answers to these questions are highly context-dependent and therefore deserving of our careful attention. Taking the time to clearly articulate the answers to these three questions will help you determine what kind of public engagement effort is required.

In the previous chapter I described a public meeting at which I was caught off guard when a member of the public asked me to explain what the decision was and who would be making it. I didn't know the answer. A few days after that meeting, I met with the project managers and decision-makers to prepare a clarification. It took us over two hours to answer the three questions. We started with, "What is the decision?" One team member said, "We're looking at options to replace a public facility." Someone else said "No, we're recommending a preferred option." And still a third said, "No, No. This is just a concept plan showing different alternatives."

Those three statements would suggest different types of projects and decisions. Was it a study? A plan? A concept? Final design and construction? And what was the actual decision? Would this project need to be accepted by one of the agencies involved? Approved by a committee? Adopted by resolution? Finally, who would be making the decision? A state agency? A local municipality? We ultimately developed a clear decision statement that we were able to communicate to the community. It was not easy, but the clarification made rest of the public engagement process a lot easier by helping us communicate to the public in a transparent manner.

#2: SET ENGAGEMENT OBJECTIVES

In her book, *The Art of Gathering: How We Meet and Why It Matters*, Priya Parker laments that the "great paradox" of meeting is that we often do it without a purpose. When we do try to develop a purpose, she points out, we often confuse categories of meetings with purpose. For instance, a networking night is intended to help people network. A book club is intended to read a book. A volunteer training is organized to train volunteers.[2]

The same is true when we plan public gatherings. We say the purpose of a public meeting is to meet with the public. The purpose of a public hearing is to hear from the public. And by that logic, the purpose of public engagement is for the public to…engage. This kind of circular thinking can cloud our reasoning and lead us to design and organize public engagement processes that lack clear objectives.

To build on this concept, we can turn to Simon Sinek's famous adage, and the name of his bestseller, *Start with Why*, in which he recommends that leaders spend time finding their purpose before moving to the "how" and the "what" of their business strategy.[3] The same is true for public engagement. Finding our "why" in public engagement is like finding our guiding light. Conversely, when we fail to uncover our reasons for embarking on a public engagement process, we end up making many of the mistakes I discuss in Chapter 4, engaging late, involving without influence, and using inappropriate techniques.

In Part 1 of this book, we learned that many of the mistakes we make in public engagement are the consequence of not defining our purpose. One of the most important steps in making public engagement easier is setting clear objectives *before* we begin to engage a community. Most planners and policymakers are familiar with the importance of setting community goals and objectives as part of the policymaking process. It is no different with public engagement. Objectives help us identify our goals clearly and tell us how to direct our efforts.

Clear objectives have a variety of benefits. First, objectives help you, as a policymaker to communicate your intentions with your team. The simple act of writing it down and discussing it with your colleagues provides an opportunity to clarify what the group wants to achieve, discuss areas of potential disagreement, and decide how to move forward.

Second, developing clear objectives helps you pick the most appropriate engagement techniques to implement during public decision process. When it comes time to decide whether it's better to host a public workshop or distribute an online survey, your objectives will guide the way. For example, if your objective is to explore perceptions of many community members, a survey is likely a good choice. However, if your objective is to discuss a series of design alternatives in-depth, you would likely select a workshop because that technique allows an exchange of ideas and information as a dialogue. A survey would not readily allow such an exchange. Objectives can help ensure you find the best technique for that situation. It's virtually impossible to pick a technique to achieve an objective that doesn't exist.

Lastly, having clear objectives helps you measure your success by providing a standard with which to evaluate your engagement plan when it's complete. In other words, did you do what you set out to do? At the end of your participation process, you can show members of your organization, funders, and the community what you accomplished and how that measures up to what you said you would do (for more on how to evaluate your process, see Chapter 12). Your engagement objectives will become a road map for the public engagement process, guiding you where you want to go, telling you if you achieved your goals at the end, and keeping you focused along the way.

Regulations are not objectives

When the parent of a five-year-old has been asked "why" a hundred times, the answer invariably becomes "because I said so." It may be the last resort, but an exhausted parent will use that response to end the discussion without having to come up with a reason. In the world of public engagement, regulations are the equivalent of saying "because I said so." But in this case, I am like the five-year-old asking my clients and partners to define why they want to do public engagement and the answer is, "Because we are required to." The danger of public engagement regulations is that the regulations can easily be substituted for purpose.

Legal requirements for direct citizen participation didn't become part of federal and state law until decades ago, with the passage of a variety of federal administrative laws. The most well-known public engagement regulations are associated with the National Environmental Policy Act (NEPA). Some states also require public engagement in certain situations, such as New York's State Environmental Quality Review Act (SEQRA) regulations and California's Coastal Act. Some other states and local governments also require public engagement.

These laws have become a necessary stopgap to ensure the public is informed about projects and initiatives. But for many municipalities and agencies, these laws have come to define their entire approach to public engagement. The minimum requirements can become the maximum effort.

We run into trouble when we treat requirements as the end goal instead of the stopgap they should be. In *Making Public Participation Legal*, Matt Leighninger writes that our legal framework for public engagement supports "only the bare minimum of deliberation." He adds that public participation laws "can stifle innovation and discourage public officials and employees from reaching out to citizens, while failing to achieve the intended goal of greater transparency."[4] Legal requirements for public engagement can be damaging because we often mistake them for purpose and objectives. If your answer to why you are doing public engagement is "because we have to," it's time to reassess.

How to set objectives

Setting quality objectives comes down to asking yourself the right questions, taking the time to answer them honestly, and including members of your team in the discussion. The time to define your engagement objectives is when you and your team are in the initial stages of a decision-making process. As we learned in previous sections, the beginning of a decision process is when you fully articulate the decision to be made. It is especially useful to include the objective-setting step while you're developing a scope of work for your project. As you refine the scope of work, the schedule, budget, and specific work tasks, take the opportunity to explore and define your engagement objectives as well.

I find it helpful to start with seven exploratory questions designed to uncover why you want to engage the community. The questions I use are intentionally broad and open-ended to provide space for reflection and brainstorming. It is important to uncover *why* you want to engage the community on this decision before jumping into the "how." I assure you that we will get to the how later. And the how will be much easier to plot out if you know why you're doing it.

To complete this exercise, you need a copy of the statement that defines your decision (i.e. what, who, and when), and a blank piece of paper or a white board. Convene your team to discuss the following questions, as a group. This is a significant opportunity to align with your team about why you want to engage the community. A brief conversation about objectives at the beginning of the decision process will help surface areas of agreement and disagreement. Getting this kind of internal understanding will make the rest of the process much easier.

Question 1: What do we hope to achieve by engaging the public in this decision? Why?

Brutally honest answers to this question may sound like the following:

I just don't want the public to call me names at a public meeting.

I want to get through it as painlessly as possible.

I want to avoid controversy. I want to get my project approved and move on.

These sentiments are normal and there is no shame in them. Give yourself the space to write them down. And then move on so you can uncover other things you may hope to achieve. This could be understanding the full range of issues, concerns, and hopes the public has about the decision. It could be that you want to ensure you can respond to at least some of the public's feedback about the decision. Maybe you want to build trust with community members and gain public support for this way of making public decisions along the way. Your answers to this question will help you connect your personal needs and desires, with the goals, needs, and realities of your team and organization. Acknowledging your personal needs and goals up front will help you stay motivated throughout the process. Anytime you feel lost or deflated, you can return to the things you wrote as an answer to this question.

Question 2: What do we want to communicate to the public? Why?

Your answers to this question will help you anticipate and gather all the information you need for overall project communications. To answer this question, start with your decision statement. At the very least, you know you want to communicate the nature of the decision, who will make the decision, and the approximate date the decision will be made.

There is other information you may want to communicate as well. You might want to communicate any pertinent background information, such as whether there were any previous studies, plans, or decisions that led to the current decision, as is case for many public decisions. There is usually a long list of previous plans, feasibility studies, scoping reports, and other decisions that paved the way for the decision at hand. You may want to communicate this history to the public.

You may also want to share pertinent technical information about your project. If it is a transportation project, you may want to share information about the status of the roadway, pavement and utilities, the width of the right-of-way, and any technical constraints to the project. If it is a flood mitigation project, you may want to share historical flood information, technical analyses completed about water flows and impacts, as well as any FEMA documentation. Regardless of the type of project, you may want to share financial information, such as how much you expect the project to cost, or any kind of financial analyses completed previously, such as benefit cost analyses or a feasibility study.

The more information you can share, the better. Often, questions, concerns, and suspicions from the public stem from a simple lack of information. So, make this list as comprehensive as possible. There are other basic pieces of information that we can forget to share unless we take the time to make a list, such as contact information for you and your staff so the public can reach you, information about how the public can get involved, as well as meeting announcements and meeting summaries.

Question 3: What hesitations do we have about engaging the public in this particular decision? Why?

If the first two questions felt like hard work, then hold onto your hats. This question is where I witness policymakers experience major breakthroughs by uncovering their fears, concerns, worries, and hesitations. If this sounds a little bit woo-woo, hear me out. Our fears can tell us a lot about our own motivations, hidden internal assumptions, and biases. Only by uncovering them can we begin to address them and make sure they don't negatively impact a public engagement process. Identifying fears can help us reframe, address, and hopefully neutralize negative feelings, biases, fears, and worries that may be blocking us from approaching the public with transparency and curiosity. Our fears and worries can block us from fully committing to engaging the public.

When answering this question, you may identify potential controversies about the decision that you and your team have become aware of. You may clarify known sticking points in the community. This may be when you identify organizations or individuals who you think are likely to oppose this decision. You may also need to unearth fears you may have about members of the community disagreeing with each other— or disagreeing with you. You may also want to identify any challenges you foresee when it comes to getting people engaged who may need support or assistance to be involved.

It is important when answering this question to make sure you include even the smallest nagging hesitations or fears. Write it all down, no matter how small, silly, or far-fetched you think it is. You don't want to wait until you're standing in front of a room of angry people to have that "ah ha" moment where you realize that it was precisely the issues you wanted to ignore that needed to be addressed early in the process.

Here's an example of why it is important to listen to your own hesitations. As part of an ongoing public engagement process in a small town, I was asked to facilitate a public meeting to discuss a controversial project in which the local municipality was going to decide whether to construct a roundabout in a residential neighborhood. Over the course of a few weeks, I worked with the decision-makers to design a public meeting. I occasionally felt a tinge of fear that members of this community would see me as an outsider. But I didn't address it. Instead, I ignored it and pushed it away, telling myself it was my professional duty to show no weakness and admit no fear. Sure enough, on the day of the meeting, some of the very first comments I received from the crowd were questions about me personally, my background, and where I came from. My outsider status was a distraction to the community and it impacted my ability to facilitate. It required more of the public's time in that meeting for me to establish credibility and trust so that the public felt comfortable sharing their own feelings about the project.

During a debrief about that meeting, I realized that little tinge of fear I felt earlier was actually a very powerful warning system. I had sensed that this community was not accustomed to outsiders. Had I taken the time to surface this fear, there are many things I could have done to address it ahead of time. First, I could have spoken about it with my client and a handful of community leaders. I could have combed through my experience working in that community so I could highlight any familiarity I had, identified aspects of the community that were similar to my own, and identified cherished local treasures, such as any restaurants, stores, or sports venues that I had patronized. I could have done additional research to make sure I knew of any unique local pronunciations of street names or other geographic markers.

I could have gone another way with it altogether and simply taken a few moments at the beginning of the meeting to address the fact that I was not from the community and explained how that was by design; that as an outside facilitator I could be an asset to the decision process because I didn't have as much of a stake in the outcome. Instead, an outsider can be solely focused on making sure the process is fair and all perspectives are heard. Any of those solutions would have made for a more authentic and effective meeting.

Our hesitations are a powerful signal that can lead us toward a productive solution. Our fears can also help us better understand what is guiding us or biasing our objectives. This is why it's important to surface our fears about engaging the public at the very beginning of the process.

Question 4: What aspects of this decision/project can be influenced
by the public?

It is critical that we can clearly articulate what aspects of a decision are actually up for discussion with the community. The reasons for that are twofold:

1. Shared influence is central to public engagement and therefore, identifying exactly how much and what kind of influence will be shared is key. In Chapter 3 we learned that without shared influence, we're not really doing public engagement. We're doing something else, such as public relations or marketing, and
2. If you can't identify any part of the decision that can be influenced by the public, that is an important thing to know early. That puts you in a perilous position and could result in unclear expectations and misunderstandings.

For those two reasons, it is imperative to document what the public can influence during the objective-setting process. When you clearly communicate what pieces of a decision the public can influence, you are building a foundation of clear expectations for the public. Having clear expectations at the outset of a decision process will make your public engagement process easier, not only for you, but also for the public.

You may be asking yourself right now, what if the public can't influence *any aspect* of this decision? There are two potential answers to this question:

1. The first answer is that sometimes we need to look closer at the project. Carefully review every aspect of a decision and make sure there truly is nothing the public can influence. Often, this requires talking over details with technical experts, such as engineers and architects. Technical experts sometimes make design decisions that appear to be based on technical requirements, when in reality there are multiple options.

2. The second way to answer this question—and only after you have an exhaustive review to determine there are truly no aspects of the decision that can be influenced by the public—is that public engagement may not be the right strategy. If there is no opportunity for influence, you should not be doing public engagement. It's possible you should be developing a public relations strategy instead—because you're trying to sell the public on the idea rather than engage in a dialogue.

Question 5: What aspects of this decision/project cannot be influenced by the public?

This question is more than just the inverse of the previous question. When my clients and partners struggle to answer what the public can influence, sometimes we will restart the discussion by instead listing the things the public *cannot* influence—and then go back over that list to reconsider each one.

Identifying aspects of a decision that cannot be influenced by the public can be uncomfortable. We don't want to admit pieces of a decision are off the table. Why? Because it's awkward and we are afraid of how the public will react. Explaining to the public what cannot be influenced is not fun especially when the decision at hand is the result of multiple previous decisions or many years in the making. To admit this means telling the public that a portion of the decision has been made or will be made by others.

On one hand, communicating this truth is an essential way to set expectations and lead a transparent process. On the other hand, telling the public they have no influence feels bad—and it also feels just a little bit untrue. Most decision-makers know in the back of their minds that the public often *does* have the final say, by virtue of protest, lobbying, or legal appeals. This knowledge can lurk in the back of our minds and make us resistant to communicating clear expectations.

Yes, it can be scary and potentially unpopular to tell the public that certain aspects of a decision have already been made, especially if those decisions were made years ago, by different decision-makers and with the input of a different generation of community members. But that makes it no less important part of setting expectations and clarifying what type of feedback you want from the public.

Question 6: What do we want to know from the public? Why?

This question comes second-to-last for good reason. We can't answer it properly until we have answered the previous five questions, until we are clear about what the public can and cannot influence. First, there is no sense in asking the public for feedback on aspects of a decision they cannot influence. Second, it is important to communicate exactly what you want to know from the public. The key to this part is to be as specific as possible. The answer to the question, "What do we want to know from the public?" should not be "We want input on the project." That request is far too vague to elicit meaningful feedback.

To help understand how to formulate our ask, let's return to the example of the Main Street redesign project. Let's say you uncovered aspects of that decision that the public may be able to influence. As part of the concept design process, the project engineers identified multiple options for configuring bicycle facilities and on-street parking. These options are nuanced and include complex trade-offs. For instance, the designers may determine there is not enough space within the existing right-of-way to provide both a protected bicycle lane and on-street parking spaces. There are options to provide *some* on-street parking, but some spaces would need to be removed to accommodate the bicycle facility.

You may need to ask for specific feedback from the public about those parking spaces. Other mini-decisions that require specific feedback could be identifying possible locations for a mid-block pedestrian crossing, the type and location of sidewalk street furniture, landscaping, decorative signage, and monument signage. These are the kinds of trade-offs for which it is helpful to seek the public's feedback, and they are among the many aspects of the design that the public could influence.

Question 7: What would a successful public engagement program look like? Why?

Congratulations! By the time you get to this question, you have done a lot of soul searching and hard work. Now you can sit back and imagine what it would be like if everything went well. This will help you visualize where you want to go and keep that at the forefront of your mind as you refine your objectives.

Does success mean everyone in the community is happy with a decision? Does it mean that the decision didn't get appealed? Or does it mean that you followed a good process? Does it mean everyone who was interested or impacted by the decision had a chance to voice their perspectives? Or that all perspectives were heard and considered? Perhaps success means that community members were able to access all pertinent information about the decision and understand how they could influence it. The important thing is to uncover what success looks like to you.

While there are key measures of a successful public engagement program (more on this in Chapter 12), what defines success to you and your team is highly context-dependent.

Understanding how you view success, at least its basic outlines, will also help you later when you evaluate your process. After all, you are not measuring the success of your engagement program relative to other communities and agencies. You're measuring your success relative to your own context, goals, and objectives.

Putting your engagement objectives together

After you (and members of your team) have answered the above seven questions, you are ready to formulate your list of objectives. The most common objectives are typically related to building awareness, sharing technical information, and seeking feedback on discrete aspects of a decision. These objectives will guide us toward certain techniques, such as creating clear communication materials and finding techniques that allow community members to provide feedback at key parts of the decision, such as in interviews, public meetings, small group exercises, or through a survey. These are all examples of techniques that are used to capture feedback at very specific inflection points in a decision process.

For an example of what engagement objectives might look like in the real world, let's consider how a town planner and her team might go about establishing engagement objectives for a local decision. In this case, let us return to the Main Street redesign project. The planner has been assigned to manage a design process, which includes directing a team of technical consultants and the internal team. In this case, the planner may want to start by outlining a few generic public engagement objectives:

- Share information about the project with the public.
- Communicate the purpose of the redesign.
- Understand the range of community member perspectives on redesigning Main Street (such as concerns, hopes and desires).
- Seek feedback from the public on the design.

In some situations, your objectives may be to have an ongoing and open dialogue with members of the public about the decision at regular intervals in the decision-making process. Such objectives would suggest that an advisory committee or community panel would be appropriate techniques. Clear participation objectives that are shared by your team will become your road map to selecting the most appropriate techniques.

For large and complex projects, or if you're working with a new team, convene a short meeting to discuss the seven questions above. It may feel like a lot to ask busy managers and decision-makers. But the time invested up front will save you countless hours later. You may avoid an embarrassing course-correct after a disastrous meeting in which you realize your objectives are very different from your team's objectives, which are, in turn, very different from the decision-makers' objectives.

You can make this step easy by documenting your participation objectives in a memo format and circulating them to your internal team and decision-makers. This is a good way to build buy-in for your eventual public engagement process. And it will be your guiding light as you proceed into the unknown.

#3: SCAN THE ENGAGEMENT LANDSCAPE - WHO IS THE "PUBLIC" AND WHAT DO THEY THINK?

Now that you have defined your decision and identified your engagement objectives, it's time to start looking outward at the wider community landscape. Just as due diligence uncovers potential issues and risks, this is the step where you take the time to understand the context that defines your particular decision before plotting out your public engagement plan. The purpose of this step is twofold: (1) to understand the range of perspectives that exist in the community and (2) to identify categories of the public and specific people to engage. This is the part of the process where you seek to answer, *"Who is the public and what do they think?"*

My clients and partners often express doubt about this step, *as "How would we possibly know what the public thinks?" and "How could we speculate?"* To which I say, "Don't speculate. Ask!"

Yes, you can come right out and ask members of the public how they feel about a potential decision before you embark on your engagement process. In most cases, community members are happy to be included at this early stage and are eager to share their thoughts with you. Not only are *you* learning, but you are simultaneously beginning the engagement process with an open mind. You're starting with a personal invitation to community members to become involved, communicating that you care what they think before you even start your project. This is powerful way to build trust.

The Engagement Scan is the key to uncovering issues and opportunities that need to be addressed in your project. Real estate developers call this due diligence. Bankers call this a risk assessment. Planners call this an existing conditions analysis. I call it an Engagement Scan because it simply means you are looking at all parts of the engagement landscape carefully. Whereas a risk assessment implies there is some lurking danger, and due diligence implies that we may uncover something that will kill a deal, a scan of the landscape is a neutral way of describing how we want to gather information before embarking on a decision process. There is no value judgment in this task.

In fact, when planning for public engagement, we want to avoid the fear/panic mindset. As we learned in Chapter 5, most of us already have a negative internal dialogue about public engagement. If we begin our process by looking for danger, then we are more likely to approach the entire process with fear. It is more productive to approach a public engagement process with an open mind and positive intent. When we call something a risk, we put a value judgment on it; that thing is "bad." Likewise, if we determine there is a "risk" that the neighbors will be outraged, we are putting a value judgment on their outrage, believing that their feelings are a threat to our decision. This puts us into an us versus them mindset. Instead, we want to approach the engagement scan with neutrality.

I call this task a scan rather than an inventory because we cannot possibly identify the concerns and expectations of every single member of a community for every single public decision. The scan is simply intended to provide us with a sampling of concerns and expectations, enough so that we have a better idea of the *range* of perspectives we may need to explore further during the engagement process.

This step is often the most perplexing for policymakers who can get stuck on the question, *How do we know what the public thinks? We're not mind readers.* It's true that none of us can read minds. But we *can* ask members of the public what they think. The goal of the scan is not to achieve statistical validity. It is simply to understand the *range* of perspectives that exist about this decision and to uncover any areas of controversy or sticking points within the community, and issues or technical topics that will need to be addressed as part of the decision-making process.

The engagement scan is a simple three-step process. It is also an iterative process, meaning that you may need to repeat the steps as you broaden your understanding of the landscape. The scan begins when you and your team identify at least six to eight individual "core" participants that will be central to completing the participation scan. You will then explore how those core participants view the decision or project at hand. You will attempt to understand the public's expectations when it comes to their involvement in the decision. After that, you will expand outwards from your core participants, and identify a comprehensive list of who you need to involve in the remainder of the engagement process.

Below I describe each of these steps in more detail.

Step 1: Develop your core participant list

In this step, you and your team will create a list of core participants, which will serve as the kernel of a larger participant database. Start with a list of the six to eight people that meet the criteria below (including people within your organization and community members outside your organization). You may be asking yourself right now, *If it is so important to include a wide variety of perspectives and types of participants, then why are you suggesting we start with such a short list of six to eight people?* This stage in the process, you are still scanning the engagement landscape. Ten to twenty people is usually the number of participants you will need to reach to gain an understanding of the key issues that surround a particular decision. It can often be less than that. The goal at this stage is not to contact every single member of the community. It is to understand the landscape. One of the most important questions you will ask during these initial interviews is, "Who else should I talk to?" Asking that will help you build from your initial list of six toward a bigger list of community leaders and other individuals who may, in turn, help connect you with their friends, family, and constituents.

Criteria for selecting core participants:
- People who have been involved in related/prior decisions.
- People who have a special interest in this decision by virtue of where they live, work, or own a business.
- People and groups who have an interest in the project because they represent youth, the elderly, or those with disabilities.

- People and groups who have been ignored or excluded from previous decisions.
- People who are likely to support the decision.
- People who are likely to oppose the decision.
- People who want to be involved.

These individuals may include neighborhood leaders, residents, representatives of advocacy organizations, elected officials, major property owners, employers, government agency representatives, and others. You may identify other criteria that are specific to your community and your type of decision.

Step 2: Conduct initial interviews with core participants

Once you have a list of core participants, you are almost ready to make contact. Before picking up the phone (yes, it is best to talk), there are a few steps you can take to ensure that you are prepared, thus demonstrating to participants that you respect their feedback and their time.

Tips for conducting initial interviews

1. Write a script. A script will help you organize your thoughts so that you don't bumble through an important first contact with key participants. A script will help you make sure you are communicating clearly about what the project/decision is, who is making the decision and when, and why you are calling this person. It's important in your script to set expectations about why you are reaching out at this time. If you have followed the steps in this book, it should be the case that you are still at the very early stages of the decision process and you are reaching out to these participants to understand the issues and opportunities *before* your organization engages the public about the decision at hand.

2. Communicate what you will do with the information you gather. Will their answers to your questions be typed verbatim and then published on the agency's website? Or will you be aggregating the results so that no one's comments will be personally attributed to them? Be sure to explain to the person how you will handle their answers and protect their personal information. It may impact how forthright they want to be and it will help you avoid revealing opinions and other information that participant expected to be confidential. See Appendix A for a sample interview script with suggested questions.

3. Send the questions to interviewees ahead of time. Providing questions ahead of time is a good way to demonstrate transparency in your process. It will allow the participant to better prepare for your conversation. I even find it helpful to include the list of questions in my initial invitation so that participants can use the questions to decide whether they want to talk with me.

4. Schedule a meeting or a call. A short phone call should be enough to move through the questions. Usually, 20 to 30 minutes should be enough. This will keep you focused while also respecting the community member's time. After all, this is only the beginning of their engagement and ideally you would like this person to stay involved throughout the process.

5. Take notes. Take very careful notes! You may need to involve a colleague to help take notes. Or you can record the conversation. If you do record, make sure you notify the community member and/ or ask for their permission to record first. Communicate what will happen to the recording when you're done.

6. Send a thank you. A thank you goes a long way toward establishing rapport. In your thank you, include a copy of your draft notes and invite the stakeholder to correct anything you may have missed or misinterpreted.

Step 3: Create your participant database

After completing initial phone calls, you now have a starting point with members of the community. Community members have shared their ideas and you have initiated an exchange of information and ideas, perspectives, concerns, and opportunities. Now you can take that information back to your team and incorporate that information into your decision-making process. The implicit promise of these interviews is that you now have a responsibility (and an opportunity) to return to those community members throughout the decision process. The interviews are thus the beginning of a two-way dialogue.

Maintaining a dialogue is as much about your intentions and hard work as it is about database management. In order to keep the dialogue going in both directions, you need a detailed list of community members. This list needs to be highly organized and easily updatable. Building an efficient, high-quality database is your only hope of keeping communications flowing. To complete this list, answer the following questions:

- **Who is impacted by this decision?** Who is most impacted will be dependent on the context of your decision, such as the location, the type and scale of the decision. This could be neighboring residents, property owners, youth, students, the elderly, employees, commuters, business owners, pedestrians, or cyclists, and many others.
- **Who is interested in this decision?** It is also important to include those who may not be directly impacted by a decision but might be interested. In the case of many development projects, transportation projects, or other site-specific decisions, this may include people who don't live or work in close proximity to the project, but may care about the community; they may visit friends and relatives; they may walk, bike, or drive through the area.
- **Who has the capacity to engage in this decision?** Understanding how various individuals and organizations can engage is an important consideration when scanning the engagement landscape. Some participants, such as representatives of government agencies, developers, or members of well-resourced advocacy organizations, have a greater ability to participate because it is likely part of their job to do so. They have a paid seat at the table. Other members of the community, such as residents, employees, youth, elderly, may have less capacity to participate because they have busy lives, with jobs and commutes, caretaking, childcare, and other obligations of daily life. Our understanding of community capacity can influence how we design an engagement process. For example, representatives of government agencies and some non-profits typically have the ability to attend multiple meetings, oftentimes during the workday. They can generally arrange for the transportation or technology necessary to attend the meeting in person or virtually. This is not the case for people who have day jobs, or do shift work, or have childcare obligations. Understanding people's various capacities to participate will help you better plan engagement activities later.
- **Who may not have been included or recognized in previous or related decisions that impact them?** In today's world, it is imperative to identify communities and individuals who have been excluded from previous decisions, even if that exclusion was the result of actions taken by your predecessors. To ensure an inclusive process, we must ensure that a diverse set of perspectives are in the room, especially people who have been excluded and ignored in the past.

Tips for creating a participant database

Many practitioners fail to communicate efficiently with the public simply because they have poor database management. Here's how to make that process easier:

- When creating your participant list, use a database tool that is easily updated and can be accessed, shared, and edited by multiple people on your team. Don't create a participant database in file that you pass around to your team via email. Put something online and set up access privileges for people on your team.
- Use one of the many available online database tools that integrate with email, web, and social media so that you can easily include a sign-up form on your project website and automate project communications, such as e-blasts and newsletters. These tools are designed by database experts so that you don't need to be a database expert. If you must create your own database, use a platform that can be shared online.
- Collect the minimum amount of information about participants that you need to communicate with them effectively. Typically, you only need someone's name and email address. We rarely need people's phone numbers and home addresses, except when working in communities without reliable internet access or with communities and groups who do not use technology or email as readily as other communities. You will gain a better understanding of these circumstances during the engagement scan. Personal information is unnecessary unless you plan to send hard copy letters and post-cards. (If you are doing a project that requires outreach to property owners, you should be working with the local government tax rolls to find addresses, anyway.) The one exception to this is for demographic information. In many cases, it is important to collect demographic information about participants to ensure that your engagement process is representative of the community. In that case, always ensure that providing demographic information is clearly optional for participants. Communicate how participants' data will be used and shared. You will also need to have a plan to ensure that personal information is protected and will remain confidential.

Keeping your database updated

Don't let your database languish simply because you don't have an efficient process for keeping it updated. Just as it is important to keep your project website updated (so that you're not advertising meeting announcements from three years ago), it is also critical to ensure that you have a system to add people to the list as the project progresses. I prefer to use a system that allows participants to sign up themselves to be on the project mailing list. I know it may seem obvious to point this out in 2023, but I still see many of my clients and partners manually enter participant contact information into a spreadsheet, which increases the likelihood of spelling errors, typos, and the risk of including people who might have attended a meeting and do not want to be on the mailing list.

Once you have developed a database of participants as part of the engagement scan, that doesn't mean it is complete and you can put it away for the rest of the project. The participant database will be constantly updated throughout the engagement program to add new people, make updates to contact information, or add other notes and information about participants that will help you better engage.

#4: WRITE A PUBLIC ENGAGEMENT PLAN

Now that you have defined your decision, set objectives, and completed a scan of the participation landscape, you are ready to write your Public Engagement Plan (PEP). The purpose of a PEP, also known as a public involvement plan (PIP) or public participation plan (PPP), is to document and communicate everything you have uncovered in the previous steps of this chapter. The PEP is a road map for your engagement process. But the real opportunity, and the strength of a PEP, is in how it can help you communicate to others in your own agency and to the public. Use a PEP as a communication tool to signal that you are undertaking a transparent decision-making process.

If you have already completed Steps 1 through 3 of this chapter, then you will already know your "why" and you will have a jump on the "who." The remaining pieces of your plan are the "what" and the "when." The PEP is your opportunity to document what kinds of participation activities you intend to implement and when. If you have done each of the previous steps in this chapter, this step will be easier. If, on the other hand, you set out to write a PPP and find that you're struggling to write the beginning sections, stop what you're doing and go back to Step 1.

The contents of your public engagement plan

Regardless of the complexity of your decision, there are a few key components that should be included in a PEP. Those components include:

- **Introduction.** An introduction to your decision, including any pertinent background information, especially if there were previous decisions leading up to and influencing the decision at hand.
- **Decision statement.** A clearly identified decision statement. It can help to put your decision statement in italics, bold, or in a text box.
- **Engagement objectives.** A section listing your engagement objectives and describe the process you used to arrive at those objectives.
- **Summary of the engagement scan.** A section summarizing what you learned during your scan of the engagement landscape. Remember to double check that you're summarizing participant's input the way you said you would (i.e. verbatim, attributed, or aggregated).
- **Engagement activities.** A section that specifies the engagement activities you plan to complete. Describe every engagement activity you intend to implement, including a website, newsletters, podcasts, public meetings, surveys, interviews, pop-ups and drop-ins, walking tours, charettes, and others. (Before you start wondering which techniques to use, hold that thought. The next chapter walks through the process of selecting the best techniques at each stage of the decision process.)
- **Communications plan.** This section identifies what kind of communication methods and tools you will use, especially if you intend to create a website, newsletters, podcasts, TV, flyers, or post-cards. The purpose of this section in the plan is to identify roles in communication. Who is responsible for sending invitations to community members? Who will be the main point of contact for questions? Who will talk to the press? The communications plan is also a good place to identify key messages, if you intend to use messaging as part of your overall process.
- **Timing and schedule.** This section should identify the timing of all participation activities relative to important decision milestones.
- **Evaluation methods.** This section identifies how you will evaluate your process (more on evaluation in Chapter 12).

Many clients ask me how long a PEP should be. My answer is: it depends. In all cases, you want the PEP to be easily understandable and accessible to a wide variety of participants. I have seen PEPs that are one page long and I have seen PEPs that are forty pages long. The length of your PEP will depend on the complexity of the project and the scale of the effort, the number of participants, and activities you propose. But please note that even if your PEP needs to be 40 pages long, be sure to organize it in a way that makes it easy for readers to navigate.

Your PEP will be a road map and a communication tool for public engagement throughout the decision process. Like many plans, it is not intended to be a static document. Rather, it is an evolving tool you will use to clarify your own thoughts, collaborate with colleagues, and find agreement with your team and decision-makers. You will likely need to redesign and re-direct your engagement activities as new information is uncovered and schedules shift. Every decision process will experience new information and other kinds of changes that require you to amend your PEP.

KEY TAKEAWAYS

1. The best way to make public engagement easier is to prepare.
2. The special collaborative nature of public engagement means that the preparation stage is also an opportunity to begin a two-way dialogue with the public.
3. The four steps in the preparation process include:

   - Define your decision.
   - Set engagement objectives.
   - Scan the engagement landscape.
   - Write a Public Engagement Plan (PEP).

4. Public engagement is rarely linear. You may need to readjust and revisit certain steps as you gain new information, or as new challenges present themselves.

REFERENCES

[1] International Association of Public Participation, *Foundations in Effective Public Participation: Planning for Effective Public Participation (Training Manual)*. 2016. p. 165.
[2] Parker, P., *The Art of Gathering: How We Meet and Why It Matters*. 2018. Penguin Publishing Group, New York City, NY.
[3] Sinek, S., *Start with Why: How Great Leaders Inspire Everyone to Take Action*. 2011. New York: Portfolio/Penguin.
[4] Leighninger, M., Making Public Participation Legal, in *Working Group on Legal Frameworks for Public Participation*. 2013.

Ten

INTRODUCTION

Finally! We made it to the part of the process where we get to pick our techniques. Techniques are the activities we use to engage with participants. A public meeting is a technique. A one-on-one interview is a technique. There are hundreds of techniques to choose from when we get to this step of the preparation process. The techniques we use in public engagement are often the most visible part of our engagement program. Meetings, workshops, and surveys tend to draw attention and make headlines. By contrast, the preparation phase is less visible because it happens before most members of the public get involved. Even decision-makers don't always see the preparation work their staff does. That's one reason many decision-makers, when faced with the prospect of engaging the community, turn first to picking the techniques.

But without preparation, we are more likely to select inappropriate techniques. For example, I was recently invited to attend a meeting among decision-makers and their staff to discuss a potential redesign of a neighborhood playground. The conversation about how to engage the community went like this:

> *Decision-maker #1: We need to engage the public on this playground rehabilitation project.*
> *Decision-maker #2: Let's hold a town hall meeting.*
> *Decision-maker #1: But first we should do a community-wide survey.*
> *Decision-maker #3: No, we should organize a charette.*
> *Decision-maker #4: What we really need is a public education campaign.*

In this example above, the decision-makers attempted to select engagement techniques before they were ready. They weren't ready because they had not yet done the preparation work; they had not found agreement

DOI: 10.4324/9781003451174-12

on what the decision was, what their engagement objectives were, who their target audience/participants were, what aspects of the decision could be influenced by the public, and what the key issues in the community were. Without knowing the answers to these questions, most of us will pick inappropriate techniques.

But if the decision-makers had prepared (as outlined in Chapter 9), they would have uncovered important information about the community that would have changed their conversation about techniques. Here's what they would have found:

- First, decision-makers would have learned that the allocated budget for playground upgrades would only allow them to replace a few pieces of equipment, rather than do complete a full redesign. Given that, a design charette would likely be overkill and lead to a lot of unmet expectations in the community.
- Second, the decision-makers would have learned that a group of residents in the surrounding neighborhood had organized a safety coalition in response to an accident that had injured a child at the playground two years ago. This group was raising private funds in hopes of creating its own design for the playground. They wanted to use private funds to install an expensive, pour-in-place rubber surface.
- Finally, decision-makers would have discovered that an adjacent neighborhood had learned of this potential playground upgrade and neighborhood leaders had vocally opposed spending public funds to upgrade a "completely satisfactory" playground when their neighborhood did not have a playground at all.

With all these issues and potentially competing goals, we can see how these decision-makers' first instinct about which techniques to use may have been inadequate. Let's imagine these decision-makers decided to proceed with the first suggestion, a town hall-style meeting. For reasons we learned in Chapter 4, a town hall-style meeting is a challenging format to use in any context. From the lack of a clear structure to the inherent power dynamics of the room arrangement, a town hall-style meeting is clearly not the right technique to use. A town hall-style meeting is more likely to frustrate participants, pit neighborhoods against each other, and generate animosity toward decision-makers. A town hall-style meeting would not allow for the kind of two-way dialogue needed to discuss a nuanced and design-oriented amenity like a playground. It's also not a good technique for anyone who intends to involve children, who are after all, the primary users of playgrounds. Town hall-style meetings don't offer appropriate opportunities for children to participate, like drawing, building models out of blocks or clay, playing games, or otherwise communicating how they like to use the playground.

Let's consider the next idea suggested by the group of decision-makers: a survey. While a community survey might be a step in the right direction, it still has many of the same limitations of a town hall-style meeting. A survey could allow community members to indicate their preferred types of play equipment and other kinds of basic preferences. But a survey would not allow a nuanced discussion about introducing a neighborhood-generated design into the project, or how to accommodate private funds. It likely would not provide an opportunity to discuss any overarching issues of equity and allocation of resources across the various neighborhoods. Aside from these issues, a survey is usually not the most effective way to communicate a project's design parameters or seek detailed feedback from the people who use the playground every day.

The example above illustrates why it is unwise to pick techniques before doing the preparation work outlined in Chapter 9. None of the three of the techniques initially suggested by decision-makers would be appropriate for the context of this decision.

Given the context of the neighborhood playground project, a more appropriate technique would be a small group discussion between local decision-makers and the neighborhood safety coalition, with the goal of learning about the community's concerns and ideas. It would also be a good time for the decision-makers to organize interviews or small group meetings with members of the adjacent neighborhood to hear about their concerns and ideas. These one-on-one and small group engagements would provide an opportunity for mutual listening, learning, and trust-building *before* key design decisions are made and *before* anyone risks their public reputation by defending a decision in front of an angry crowd.

Selecting the right techniques for each stage of a decision-making process comes down to two key concepts: (1) start small, and (2) align techniques with each step in a decision.

START SMALL

Starting small is an effective way to manage group dynamics throughout a complex decision-making process. Even so, many decision-makers do the opposite. Local leaders are tempted to begin a public engagement process with a big, splashy kick-off meeting for the entire community. Starting big can be appealing to local leaders because it gives the impression of being efficient, inclusive, and fair. But starting with a large meeting can have the opposite of the intended effect.

When we convene a large group at the beginning of a decision process, we are arbitrarily inviting people to participate who have varying levels of interest in the project; people who may be impacted in very different ways. Consider that this large, kick-off meeting will be most people's introduction to the project and their first interaction with decision-makers. At this meeting, we blend the most impacted people in the room together with people who may only have a passing interest in the project. We may have brought people in the room with little capacity to participate, together with people who may have financial backing from well-funded organizations. Most likely, we won't know who is who because we haven't spoken with anyone yet. Perhaps we are meeting them for the first time on the night of the large meeting. While local leaders may think that gathering everyone together in this manner is efficient and fair, the meeting participants may not agree.

Consider the perspective of a community member who is most impacted by a decision. Upon arriving at the meeting, such participants may notice immediately that they have been lumped together with every other kind of interested party—that decision-makers somehow think their concerns are on the same level as everyone else's. Feeling disrespected and ignored, those people may conclude they must fight to be heard. Instead of starting a decision process in a collaborative tone, the big, community kick-off meeting may instead activate people's defenses and send a signal that it's time for them to prepare for battle.

A big meeting should not be your first contact with members of the community who are most impacted by a decision or with people who may not have the capacity to sustain participation through a long decision-making process. Instead, I recommend that local leaders start with small group techniques at the beginning of a decision process. Engage with individuals and small groups of people first, and then work your way toward successively larger groups of people.

The advantages of starting can be summarized as follows:

- Starting small gives you a chance to build rapport with the most interested and impacted community members *before* convening a large group at a potentially contentious public meeting.

- Starting small shows respect for the most impacted or interested participants by engaging them first, before broadening the process to people who may only have a passing interest in the decision.
- Starting small helps you understand key issues and concerns early, which means you may have a chance to address those issues before broadening engagement to larger groups.
- Starting small can help you prevent surprises from cropping up as you broaden engagement to larger groups and to broader cross-sections of a community. (Avoiding surprises at public meetings is not simply a self-serving concept. Dealing with surprises at public meetings can throw an entire meeting off-kilter, create unnecessary conflict, and can cause a meeting to be ended early.)

ALIGN TECHNIQUES WITH EACH STEP IN A DECISION

In Chapter 8, we learned how decision science can make public engagement easier. All we need to do is follow a multi-step rational decision-making process and align our public engagement techniques with each step. "Hold on," you may be thinking, "that doesn't sound easy." That's why I have included a simple way to group the decision-making process into stages that naturally align with different public engagement techniques.

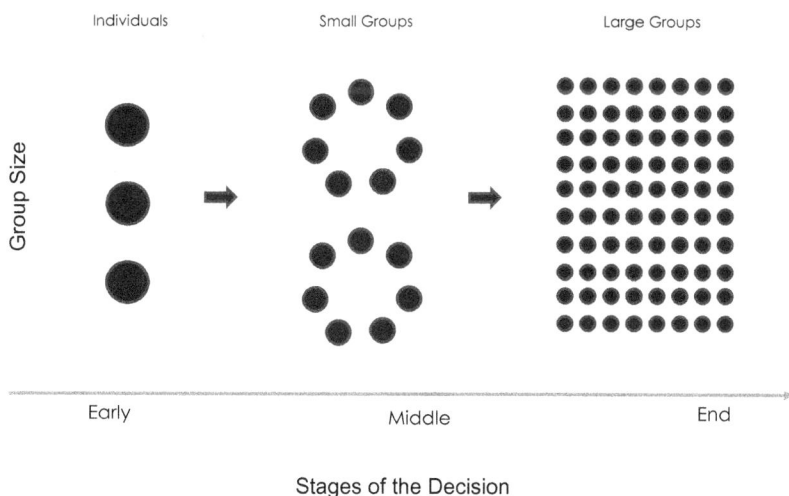

Figure 10.1 Small to large groups. Starting with small group interactions at the beginning of a decision-making process provides an opportunity for you to recognize and elevate the most impacted and interested members of the community before convening larger groups.

One of the most important things to remember when selecting engagement techniques is this: *when* you execute is as important, if not more important, than *what* you execute. When implemented very early in a decision process, engagement techniques you may consider conventional, standard, or boring can be incredibly effective, simply by virtue of when they were implemented. The inverse is also true: the most creative, interactive, fun, and inclusive workshop ever designed won't be very effective if you wait until too late in the decision process to host it. The figure below is organized on a timeline: the typical six-step decision-making process is divided into three phases: early, middle, and end. Each phase includes examples of techniques that work well within each phase (Figure 10.2.).

Techniques for the early phase
- **Phase: Early**

- **Step 1: Identify the problem**
- **Step 2: Analyze existing conditions**

The goal of public engagement early the public decision process is to build awareness about a decision and identify key issues and opportunities. At this stage, it is likely that you will want to push information more broadly to larger groups of the community while gathering feedback from a relatively small segment of the community. Many members of the community

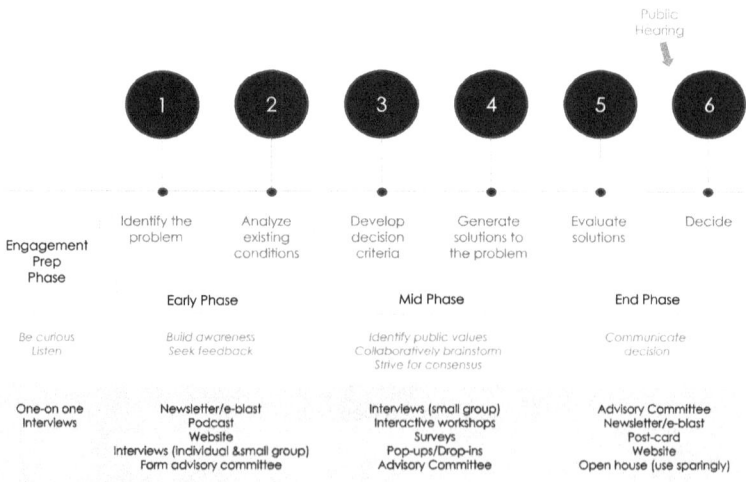

Figure 10.2 Effective alignment with engagement techniques.

may not yet be aware of the project or the decision to be made. There is some basic information you need to share so that members of the community have the ability to decide if and how much they want to be involved.

Techniques convenors can use to push information to large numbers of people in the community include:

- Project website
- Post-card/letter
- Newsletter
- Podcast
- Social media
- Press release
- TV and radio news media

At the same time, it is important to continue the momentum of the engagement activities you began during the Engagement Scan by continuing a two-way dialogue with smaller groups, starting with those who are most impacted or interested in the decision. These kinds of conversations will allow you to share key background information about the project and seek feedback about existing conditions, issues, opportunities, and decision criteria. Ways to seek feedback from small groups within the community include the following techniques:

- Structured one-on-one interviews
- Small group interviews
- Formation of an advisory committee or a citizen jury[1]

Public engagement techniques implemented during the initial stages of a public decision process should focus on individuals and smaller groups to help build rapport, trust, and identify issues and concerns. Don't mistake this as somehow doing less public engagement. The beginning stages of the process may be the most intensive phases of the entire engagement program.

Techniques for mid-way through a decision process
- **Phase: Middle**

- **Step 3: Develop decision criteria**
- **Step 4: Generate solutions to the problem**

After you have identified the problem, developed a scope of work, and gathered existing conditions, your decision process has advanced toward its middle phases, which includes two important steps: develop decision criteria and generate solutions to the problem. Because you have already engaged individuals and small groups in a structured way to help understand key issues and opportunities, you are now ready to broaden your techniques to larger groups.

These two decision phases involve idea generation, making them ideal opportunities to engage the community in brainstorming and prioritization. Given where these phases are positioned within the overall decision-making sequence, and the nature of the subject matter, these phases are well-suited for medium-to-large group activities, such as public workshops (in-person or online), surveys, and pop-ups.

Developing and ranking decision criteria

Decision criteria are an essential decision-making aid. Clear criteria can help decision-makers communicate principles, standards, and parameters with the public, which is a powerful way to increase transparency. Decision criteria can also be an expression of community values. Likewise, shared values are the building blocks of successful public decision-making.

In every public decision-making process, local leaders need to decide how they are going to make the decision. Criteria are the factors used by organizations to help make their decisions. In the public sector, we often refer to criteria as "goals" and "objectives" or "standards." Regardless of the term we use, all public decisions should be made with the aid of some kind of criteria.

It is generally better to develop decision criteria early in a decision process—and before you have generated solutions (or alternatives) to the problem. Certain points in the decision-making process lend themselves better to the criteria development process. For instance, you don't want to develop decision criteria too soon in a decision process because you will not have had the chance to gather pertinent information about the existing conditions, issues, and opportunities. You also don't want to create decision criteria too late, such as *after* the decision is made.

Post-decision criteria development happens more than you might think. I have seen many decision-makers scramble to develop decision criteria after making a decision. As we learned in Chapter 4, this is the classic "decide-announce-defend" model of decision-making (DAD), where a government body makes a decision and then produces criteria afterwards to help defend the decision they already made. I do not recommend local leaders develop decision criteria to defend a predetermined decision. The DAD model creates frustration and resistance among the public. It is the opposite of transparency and can have negative impacts on public trust.

If you have limited resources and time to devote to public engagement, you can maximize your impact by engaging the community in the process of developing decision criteria during the early and middle stages of the decision-making process. Here are three key steps:

Step 1: Develop and share draft decision criteria with the public
You may already have decision criteria and you just don't know it. Technical standards, policy goals, regulatory constraints, and legal requirements are all inputs into your decision criteria. You can call them "givens," "standards," "guidelines," or "technical criteria." Existing criteria should be the low-hanging fruit because it's likely the community has already participated in creating them. In many cases, your organization may be subject to factors beyond local control, such as eligibility for federal grants. Such factors should be incorporated into existing decision criteria.

In many communities, existing criteria include things like technical design standards, goals and objectives in a Comprehensive Plan, or recommendations from a community design workshop. Look for goals, policies, and standards within existing planning documents that are relevant to the decision at hand. Such criteria are a natural starting point for a discussion with the community. Sharing existing criteria with the public at this stage of the decision-making process is a good way to establish parameters and set expectations around your decision.

Step 2: Invite the public to brainstorm other criteria
After you have shared your pre-existing criteria and givens, you are ready to discuss additional factors that may be important to the community. This is a magical step in the engagement process, as it is your chance to incorporate the community's values into a decision-making process. The more people see their values reflected in a public decision, the more likely they are to accept that decision. In that way, this step is also another opportunity to understand concerns, issues, and values early in the decision process. The more we know about people's

concerns and hopes early in the process, the more time we must address them before making a decision.

Step 3: Invite the public to rank the decision criteria
It is not always necessary to rank or apply weighting to decision criteria, but it can help balance opposing or conflicting criteria. Ranking decision criteria can be helpful in complex projects that have many technical parameters and standards, or conditions that require trade-offs. For instance, street rehabilitation projects usually contend with limited right-of-way widths, which forces a trade-off between various desired street components, such as sidewalks, on-street parking, bike lanes, and vehicle travel lanes. In those cases, it is helpful to rank the importance of criteria to help facilitate the decision. Decision criteria in many can represent conflicting direction. For instance, "preserve on-street parking" and "ensure there are protected bike lanes" are two potentially conflicting goals if both features cannot fit into the existing street. In that case, using ranked criteria can help clarify priorities in an objective manner.

There are a variety of ways to rank decision criteria depending on the complexity of the decision at hand. One of the simplest ways to rank criteria involves ordering the criteria from least to most important, giving each criterion a rating (for example from 1 to 10). Pairwise ranking (or pairwise comparison) is a more complex method of ranking. It involves ranking criteria by comparing them in a series of head-to-head pair votes. Think of a visual preference survey in which participants select their preference among a series of choices, each offering two pictures compared to each other. Whether using simple or complex ranking systems, take advantage of software and online tools to facilitate the ranking process.

The two middle phases of a decision process represent an opportunity to broaden engagement to larger groups. In addition, the process of discussing criteria and generating solutions is most suited to two-way dialogue. Collaborative techniques that are especially helpful for discussing decision criteria and development of solutions include:

- Interactive public workshop
- Online survey
- Pop-ups (examples of pop-ups include a booth at a farmer's market or a table at a festival)
- Meeting-in-a-box (a meeting kit created by decision-makers that contains everything a community organization would need to

convene and host their own public meeting. When completed, community organizations send the results to decision-makers)
• Leverage existing community organization meetings (decision-makers may opt to attend existing/regular meetings of community organizations to share information)

Techniques for the end of a decision-making process
• **Phase 5: Evaluate Options**
• **Phase 6: Decide**

By the time you reach the later phases of a decision process, you will already know what the community's key issues and opportunities are, and you will already have sought feedback from the community about other major milestones, such as decision criteria and potential solutions to the problem. At this point in the decision process, any additional feedback you seek should be related to small details in the decision, rather than anything that would require you to reverse course. In other words, there shouldn't be any surprises at this stage.

During these phases, it is important to focus your efforts on timely and efficient communication. After completing an intense round of engagement in previous phases of the decision, many practitioners feel they have enough feedback to move forward. Many are simply tired. Either way, meaningful follow-up with the community can easily get lost in the final stages of a decision. But it is still a critical time to maintain regular communication with the public. Community members need to know what happened with their feedback. They need to know you listened. Regular e-blasts and newsletters are effective ways to keep community members informed. Communications at this stage in the decision-making process should address the following questions: (1) What did we hear? (2) How did community input influence the decision? (3) What comes next?

The final stage of decision process is one of the few instances I might recommend an open house meeting. An open house meeting provides an opportunity to share large amounts of information with the public while also allowing the public to choose what information they want to know. An open house meeting also offers flexibility for attendees who may want to drop in for a few minutes but may not have time to sit through a two-hour meeting.

That said, hosting an open house is a tight rope walk. Don't let an open house turn into a town hall-style meeting—and avoid the temptation of adding a PowerPoint presentation to an open house meeting format. A formal presentation generally requires an opportunity for Q&A. And any gathering that offers a presentation and a Q&A starts to look less like an open house and more like a different kind of gathering. Remember that any time we convene the public, we create an expectation among attendees that there will be opportunities for discussion and feedback. If your goal is to communicate one-way information, consider ways to achieve that without convening the public.

Techniques to use at the end phases of a decision-making process:

- Website/social media updates
- Newsletter
- Podcast
- E-blast
- Public hearing
- Open house

KEY TAKEAWAYS

Techniques are the activities we use to engage with participants. Selecting the right techniques for each stage of a decision-making process comes down to two key concepts:

1. **Start small.** A big, splashy public meeting should not be your first contact with members of the community who are most impacted by a decision or with people who may not have the capacity to sustain participation through a long decision-making process. Engage with individuals and small groups of people first, and then work your way toward successively larger groups of people.

2. **Align techniques with each step in a decision.** Certain techniques are better suited to each phase of a typical decision-making process (early, middle, and end). For instance, don't wait until the very end of your decision process to host a brainstorming workshop. Similarly, an online survey distributed too soon in a decision process may confuse community members who have not yet been introduced to the project.

NOTE

1. Citizen juries are a popular form of small group deliberation. A citizen jury is formed from a representative sample of community members (usually selected in a random or stratified manner) who are briefed in detail on the background and current thinking relating to a particular issue or project. The jury is asked to consider the alternatives and recommend the most attractive alternative for the community.

Eleven

INTRODUCTION

In previous chapters, we learned which public engagement techniques pair best with each phase of a decision-making process. But knowing when to conduct an interview and when to host public workshop still leaves questions about what to do during those gatherings. Many of my clients and partners are not expert facilitators and don't have experience running group discussions. They often ask me, "What do I actually *do* at these gatherings?"

If you search the internet for meeting exercises, you may be overwhelmed to find a long list of techniques, many of which may seem too advanced for you and your team. There is a time and a place for advanced facilitation techniques. You may decide at some point that you want to hire an expert facilitator to help you with a particularly complicated public discussion. But if you're like most of my clients and partners, you and your team are responsible for planning and executing the majority of public engagement activities in your community. You need a handful of go-to facilitation techniques that are effective, yet affordable and practical. This chapter includes five facilitation techniques that are easy and inexpensive to implement, whether you're hosting an in-person or virtual event. You don't need to become an expert facilitator to accomplish these techniques.

THE POWER OF PRODUCTIVE VENTING

When we ask members of the public to take time out of their busy lives to come to a meeting or event, it is important to demonstrate that we value their time and input. Unfortunately, many public meetings are not structured in a way that allows the public to share their concerns. Many public meetings start with a long PowerPoint presentation. In Chapter 3, we learned why this is not a good idea and here's why: The more time we spend presenting, the

DOI: 10.4324/9781003451174-13

less time the public must share ideas. The more data we present, the more it looks like we have already decided the best course of action.

A powerful way to change the dynamic is to provide opportunities for the public to interact and give feedback as soon as they arrive at a meeting. When a participant walks in the door (or signs into an online meeting), give that person an opportunity to say something meaningful right away. The most important thing to ask is why; Why did they take the time out of their day to come to this gathering? What drew them to the meeting and why is the decision at hand important to them?

People go to public meetings for many reasons, but mostly because they have an opinion about something. By the time someone finds themselves at a public meeting, it's likely they have already formed a position on the decision at hand. Our goal is to help participants unpack their positions as soon as they walk into the room. We want to shift their mindsets away from positions and toward values as soon as we can. The way to do this is with a productive venting exercise.

Productive venting involves two key questions:

- "What drew you to this meeting?"
- "Why is this issue important to you?"

If you think the idea of asking members of the public to answer these questions in a public meeting sounds like opening the pandora's box, you're not alone. Many of my clients resist the idea of such a direct approach. It seems counterintuitive if the goal is to keep control of a public meeting.

We don't want to encourage negativity.

What if people say horrible things?

Isn't it counter-productive to invite disagreement before we even get started?

Of course, we don't want to create a negative atmosphere. But does asking those questions *create* negativity? Or does asking the questions simply uncover issues that were already there (and are likely to emerge at some point, anyway)?

Let's consider the real cause of negativity. Chapter 5 introduced an important concept from Peter Sandman's book, *Responding to Community Outrage*. That is, if people are not already concerned about an issue or proposal, what is the risk that asking how they feel about it will cause concern that wasn't there to begin with?[1] Asking people how they feel about a particular issue is not going to *cause* negativity. If there is negativity, it was already there before. And it will come out eventually.

To help understand how productive venting can help, let's first consider a scenario where the public did *not* have chance to productively vent. In this example, I was asked to help a group of local officials with damage control after a disastrous public meeting. They had undertaken a project with the goal of improving the safety of an intersection in a residential neighborhood. One option was to replace the four-way stop sign with a roundabout.

Knowing the topic might be controversial, the officials arrived at the public meeting armed with traffic studies, safety studies, and design concepts proving how much safer a roundabout would be than a four-way stop sign. But many of the neighbors who attended the meeting felt that roundabouts were unsafe. Others felt they were a waste of taxpayer dollars. Before the officials got through the first five minutes of their presentation, members of the crowd interjected with questions, skepticism, and hostility. Feeling attacked, the local officials became defensive about their work and simultaneously tried to assure the crowd that roundabouts were the safest option. But the more they assured the crowd, the less the crowd believed them. Soon, some members of the audience began to talk among themselves and grumble. Others booed and yelled at the presenters. Still others walked out in disgust. The local officials were forced to end the meeting early and retreat.

I have witnessed versions of the above scenario many times. Afterward meetings like that, local officials scratch their heads and wonder, *What went wrong? Why are people so unreasonable? If people would just listen to facts, then they would agree with our thinking.*

In the world of public decisions, we often rush to present a message before listening to the community's core beliefs and values. We, as practitioners and public officials, don't usually give the public a chance to share their concerns and ideas before we push talking points, facts, and figures. And often we find out later that our talking points and data were in direct conflict with community's core beliefs and values. In the example I described above, the community expressed values around safety and a desire for a limited role of government. But those values were obscured because the meeting format did not allow for an open discussion.

When local officials and subject matter experts are faced with intense scrutiny at a public meeting, many naturally become defensive and overreliant on evidence. To protect their own investment of time and energy, they convince themselves that the public is simply irrational, ignorant, and rude. We call them NIMBY's, or worse.

Blaming the public for feeling unheard is unproductive and ignores fundamental principles of human emotion and cognition. We cannot combat outrage by ignoring people's feelings or by trying to bulldoze them with facts. The solution is not to withhold data and evidence from the public. Rather, the way forward is to first listen to the community's concerns. Take their concerns seriously with an understanding that those concerns are based on lived experience. Only after listening can we ask the public to consider our evidence and data.

This is where productive venting can help. The exercise allows people to share their feelings, concerns, and ideas. Disclosing stress (positive venting) is an effective coping mechanism. People feel immediate relief from airing grievances. It helps create acceptance and insight for the person venting. There are also benefits to the person (or people) listening. When someone shares what is on their mind, the listener gains connection, focus, and perspective.

A hallmark of public consensus involves identifying and addressing concerns about a decision early in the process. To that end, productive venting is a consensus-building activity. When we give people an opportunity to share concerns at the beginning of a public decision-making process or a meeting, we can acknowledge their feelings at the outset. Participants are more likely to feel heard and validated. Having heard their concerns repeated aloud or seeing their concerns written on paper, participants will be more able to listen to a technical presentation, rather than using that time to formulate arguments. In short, participants will be much more open to the information you share *after* they have a chance to do some productive venting.

How to implement productive venting

I advise my clients to build in opportunities for productive venting at any gathering, whether meeting in person or online. The key is to do this exercise before giving a presentation or sharing any evidence or data with meeting participants. The short activity described below can be offered to meeting participants as soon as they walk in the door or directly after they have signed in (or in the case of virtual meetings, as soon as they are admitted to the meeting).

- At the sign-in table (or on the screen for an online meeting), create a small display that is easily visible to participants entering the room. The display includes a large piece of paper or a white board. Also make sure you have sticky notes, index cards, tape, and markers available.

- Write the following two questions on the white board or on a piece of butcher paper.

  - "What drew you to this meeting today?"
  - "Why is this issue [insert project name] important to you?"

- As participants arrive and sign-in, invite them to consider and answer the questions, using a sticky note, or by writing directly on the wall/whiteboard.
- Give participants a few minutes to consider an answer, perhaps while they settle into a seat and enjoy refreshments you provided.
- Ask each participant to return their answers to you or tape them to the wall.
- Encourage participants to review other people's answers.

What to do with the results of productive venting

Productive venting is not just a touchy-feely exercise intended to placate a crowd. It is a chance for the convenors to understand issues and concerns in the room and address them. Addressing issues and concerns doesn't mean you have to solve them in the moment. It simply means acknowledging they exist.

After completing this exercise, convene the meeting and spend a few minutes reviewing the responses out loud to the group. Ask if anyone would like to add anything. Don't be afraid to read responses that are critical. Your willingness to do that shows the audience that you're willing to acknowledge how people feel.

This activity allows you to acknowledge and validate people's beliefs and values, which will help them relax and shift out of an emotional state. In my experience, most people are delighted to be asked their opinion within 20 seconds of walking into the meeting. This activity gives them a chance to settle into the meeting and be in the moment. This will also provide you, as the meeting host, a great opportunity to understand who is in the room and what is important to them.

In addition, participants have a chance to see other people's responses. There will likely be overlap and commonalities in their responses, which will help community members build rapport and trust with each other, as well. At the end of the exercise, you will have a written record of participants' feedback.

Productive venting is a useful exercise for almost any gathering. It can be used during one-on-one interviews and small group discussions.

It is especially useful for large groups as a first point of contact when participants arrive to a meeting.

FIST TO FIVE

Unless there is an actual referendum on the table, I try to avoid exercises that look like voting. Voting exercises can create a false expectation among the public that they are really voting on an actual decision itself. And while we want to avoid false expectations, most policymakers understand that voting exercises, like dot exercises and surveys, are a popular way to gauge the opinions of a group quickly. People generally understand how to vote and voting exercises are generally simple to implement.

The Fist to Five technique helps bridge the gap between pure voting exercises and consensus-building activities.[1] Fist to Five works well when you want to check in with a group and gauge their level of agreement with an idea or the general direction of a discussion. It is especially helpful if a few people in the room have dominated the discussion, or if some people are especially quiet.

The Fist to Five exercise works by asking everyone in the room to raise their hands and use their fingers to indicate their level of agreement with a proposal or potential decision. The levels of agreement are:

- Closed fist: A firm no. "I will block this decision if I can."
- One finger: "I have significant concerns about this proposal and we should address them immediately."
- Two fingers: "I have minor issues that need attention."
- Three fingers: "I don't love this, but I'm okay letting it pass and then resolving the problems later."
- Four fingers: "This proposal is workable, so I'm in favor."
- Five fingers: "This proposal is excellent, and I will champion it."

The point of this exercise is not to count the exact number of fingers raised and tally up the votes. Rather, it is an easy way for a facilitator to scan the room and get a general sense of agreement or disagreement. This exercise has a powerful effect on participants, too. It is a subtle way to enable nuance and to suggest there are varying levels of agreement or disagreement. Participants don't need to hold tight to a yes/no position when they see there is a scale of options beyond that. Having the option to disagree without having to say "no" to the entire proposal can empower participants to engage in more productive discussion.

This exercise offers many of the benefits of voting (it's quick and easy) but also provides some of the nuance of a consensus-building activity. When facilitating large groups where it's hard to see everyone's hands, you can implement this technique using polling software, color-coordinated auction paddles, or by asking people to move around the room into spaces representing each of the five categories.

HOW TO UPGRADE YOUR COMMENT CARD

Many planners and policymakers have a love/hate relationship with comment cards. Comment cards are easy to implement. Comment cards don't require anyone to have advanced facilitation techniques, nor do they require challenging conversations with participants. More importantly, comment cards allow policymakers to avoid getting yelled at. But comment cards have downsides. They are both the cause and result of unclear expectations in public engagement. Leaving a comment is not an especially empowering activity for members of the public; it is the opposite of having a dialogue. By definition, a comment card asks simply for "comments," rarely explaining what those comments should address. Members of the public who fill out a comment card may not have any idea what exactly their comments should address.

A comment card implies a vague request, signaling to stakeholders that we don't really care what they think and that we don't intend to do anything with their feedback. Sure, a comment card lets members of the public say anything they want. But a comment card is evidence that policymakers haven't taken the time to explain to stakeholders what aspects of the decision can be influenced, therefore what exactly the public should comment on.

Imagine a member of the public trying to sift through a 140-page policy document and figure out how to comment: *Should I comment on the demographic analysis? On the policies? On the font? What are they going to do with my comment?* If you want to signal to the public that you really care about their feedback, comment cards need to be specific. If you do it well, you can use your comment card to do some amazing things. You can use this seemingly conventional request to increase transparency around your decision, get better quality feedback, and save people's time.

Tips for how to upgrade your comment card
- Include your decision statement on the back of the comment card (see Chapter 9 for a description of how to define your decision).

- Indicate what aspects of the decision the public can influence—and ask for feedback on those aspects.
- Offer options and choices where possible to show your understanding of the key issues and range of ideas that the public have already offered.
- Make your ask-for comments as specific as possible. For example:

  - *What do you like about Comprehensive Plan Goal #4? What do you not like?*
  - *In what ways do you think this streetscape project will achieve (or not achieve) the goal of greater accessibility for disabled community members along Main Street?*

- Don't ask for comments on aspects of the decision the public cannot influence.

BETTER WAYS TO BRAINSTORM

The early stages of many public decisions involve a period of brainstorming for ideas, opportunities, and solutions. Whether it is for visioning, goal setting, or identifying challenges and opportunities, policymakers need effective techniques to help groups of people generate ideas. Enter the brainstorm. A typical brainstorm might involve a large group of people and someone at the front of the room with a flip chart. A facilitator may start by asking a question. People in the room may call out ideas. Facilitators say, "there are no bad ideas in brainstorming." But there are some downsides to traditional brainstorming. First, if it is a large group of people (over 20), not everyone will feel comfortable sharing their ideas. In other cases, there won't be time for everyone to share their ideas. Traditional brainstorming can also lead to groupthink, as participants try to coalesce around an idea (consciously or unconsciously).

An alternative way to brainstorm with a group is through a technique called Cardstorming. Cardstorming is a technique that combines individual reflection and group discussion.

Here's how it works

- A facilitator asks meeting participants to quietly consider a question and then write the answers to that question on an index card or a sticky note.
- When each person is done reflecting and writing their answer, they can post their answers to the wall.
- When everyone is done posting their answers to the wall, the facilitator gathers the group around the display of responses to review

what everyone wrote. The facilitator highlights commonalities and differences observed in the feedback.

- The facilitator can even engage the group in a discussion of conclusions, priorities, and action items.
- Note: this activity can be implemented using online/digital tools.

Cardstorming overcomes some of the challenges of traditional brainstorming. Many people need time to think before they jump into an exercise of generating ideas with a group. The Cardstorming technique gives participants a few minutes of quiet time, alone, to consider their responses to questions. The alone time helps combat groupthink by encouraging everyone to generate their own ideas before hearing everyone else's. Cardstorming also offers the opportunity for participants to choose whether they remain anonymous. If someone chooses to post their response to the wall, they can decide whether to share that it was their idea. If, on the other hand, that person wants everyone to know it was their idea, they can put their name on it or be sure to speak up when the group is convened for discussion. In this way, everyone can share ideas more freely.

Cardstorming allows participants to see what everyone else said. Once everyone's ideas are posted to the wall, it's easy for participants to see everyone else's ideas, options they hadn't considered, and differences of opinion. People feel more at ease when they can see feedback similar to their own. Likewise, meeting participants are more able to consider alternative ideas with an open mind—even when they disagree.

Once everyone has had a chance to scan other people's responses, the facilitator can invite the full group to stand and gather around the cards on the wall. This is where the magic happens. Most participants are glad for the chance to get out of their chairs and move around. This is a great way to lighten up the atmosphere in the room and change the power dynamic between the facilitator and the group. At this point, the facilitator can engage the group by asking if anyone sees commonalities in the responses. When people point them out, the facilitator (or a volunteer) can shuffle the cards around to place similar themed ideas together.

Moving the cards around in real time provides visual evidence to participants of where common ground exists, where new ideas have emerged, and where there may be disagreement. The facilitator can ask the group if those who wrote these cards would like to say more about why they wrote what they did. After addressing commonalities, the facilitator may ask if anyone sees areas of conflict or disagreement. These, too, can be placed together on the wall to help participants see how the ideas are unfolding.

I have seen participants of Cardstorming exercises more readily shift positions about topics after seeing and hearing how others view the issue, especially if it helps the group come to agreement. At the same time, if someone feels strongly about a topic, this technique offers the opportunity to discuss it in a productive way.

Cardstorming offers the following benefits:

- Allows everyone some time to think on their own before answering a question.
- Provides an unfiltered, visual representation of the group's ideas, commonalities, and differences.
- Allows people who are not comfortable speaking in front of a group to present their ideas on equal footing with everyone else's.
- Participants can choose their level of anonymity by publicly "claiming" their ideas to the group or by remaining anonymous.
- Invites participants out of their seats.
- Creates a collaborative, teamwork atmosphere that breaks through the typical speaker/audience power dynamic of a public meeting.
- Allows ideas posted to the wall to be moved around, making categorization and prioritization easy to do in real time.
- Provides a visual representation of the group's ideas.

Cardstorming is a great tool for visioning, goal setting, and prioritization. An important part of the technique is designing the right questions. When using Cardstorming for a visioning exercise, use creative and open-ended prompting questions that help uncover participant's values instead of encouraging them to narrow their answers into fully formed positions. For example, for a discussion about a community's future vision, don't ask "What should the vision for our town be?" Instead, ask any or all the following questions:

- Why did you choose to live here?
- When you think about your town, what makes you feel most safe/happy/proud?
- What is important to you about our town's future and why do you care?

- In 25 years, how would you want your grandchildren to describe this town to their friends?

"Q-storming"

Question-storming (Q-storming) is like brainstorming. But instead of brainstorming answers to questions, participants brainstorm questions. While this technique may not be appropriate for every project or context, it is useful in certain situations. It is most useful at the very beginning stages of a decision-making process, even before the problem or the project has been fully defined. It is also useful for highly complex or controversial projects because it allows participants with wildly different perspectives, backgrounds, and levels of expertise to work together on a problem without the pressure of generating solutions.

During traditional brainstorming, there is subtle pressure to come up with a "good idea." As a result, many people hold back on contributing because they are afraid they won't offer a winning idea. Q-storming removes the need to offer the "right" answer. The point of the exercise is to generate questions, encouraging participants to approach the exercise with an open mind and think of a problem from many angles.

For this reason, Q-storming is a good technique when the problem at hand is complex or can be defined in multiple ways. Many types of planning projects are well-suited to the Q-storm technique, including housing strategies, climate action plans, comprehensive plans, strategic plans, feasibility studies, and transportation plans.

Q-storming can be implemented using the same method as Cardstorming. Instead of asking participants to answer a question, start with a problem statement and ask participants to identify as many questions as they can about the problem.

- Start out with a problem statement.
- Then ask: "What question, if answered, could make the greatest difference to the future of the situation?"

You can facilitate a Q-storming exercise with individuals, small groups, and large groups. You can even combine the Cardstorming technique with Q-storming, so that participants consider their questions and write them on cards before discussing with the larger group. At the end of a Q-storming exercise, you will have a list of questions that will help you refine a problem. The results of a Q-storming exercise will also reveal a lot about how community members think about the problem, including values, concerns, and ideas.

THE POWER OF SMALL GROUPS

The benefit of small group work, particularly in educational settings, has been widely accepted since the 1970s. People working in small groups develop deeper understanding of issues. They learn more and retain more information. Small group participation can broaden a discussion by encouraging shy or reluctant participants to speak up and by preventing anyone from dominating a conversation. Small group work has been shown to help students develop collaborative skills, which allows them to share diverse perspectives, develop empathy, pool knowledge, hold each other accountable, and solve more complex problems than participants would be able to on their own.[2–5]

Benefits of small group discussion

- Small groups give more opportunity for "talk time" than large meetings, where only a few people may have the opportunity to speak for a defined number of minutes.
- Small groups encourage sharing of ideas, especially among people who are not comfortable sharing in a large group.
- Small groups create synergy. Synergy is a gain in performance when a group of people create a combined result that is greater than the sum of their separate results, or a result that is beyond what any one person could achieve by working on a problem alone.[2]
- Small groups can increase motivation. Working with others on a task-directed activity can increase participants' understanding and motivation.

How to organize small group discussions

Small group exercises are relatively easy to orchestrate in a variety of public gatherings, whether in-person or virtual meetings (the major virtual meeting platforms include breakout room features, which are the virtual equivalent tables of small groups).

Key considerations for organizing small group discussions:

- Provide clear instructions for the discussion to the entire room before breaking into smaller groups.
- Provide written instructions on each table, including questions you would like the group to discuss and answer.

- For more complicated discussions, consider placing a table facilitator at each table. You do not need professional facilitators for this. The table facilitator's job is to make sure everyone understands the instructions and keep the discussion moving. Table facilitators can be members of your team, students, or volunteers. If you don't have access to extra people to act as facilitators, you can ask each table/group to nominate someone at the table to be a volunteer facilitator.
- If you have enough staff, place a note-taker at each table. Like the facilitator, if you do not have enough staff, ask each table to nominate a note-taker.
- Provide a recording template, such as a pre-printed sheet with maps and questions you would like the group to answer. Provide prompts for the note-taker.
- Seat no more than eight to ten people around each table (either round or rectangular tables).
- Walk around the room to monitor each group's discussion. If you see a group that is overly quiet or not taking notes, intervene to help restart conversation. (Virtual meeting platforms allow the hosts to drop in and out of breakout groups to monitor discussions.)
- Avoid the typical "report out" after small group discussions have concluded. Typical report-outs drag on far too long and involve repetition. If you have asked each group to take careful notes, you won't need a detailed report out of each group. Instead, when you convene the full group, review the prompting questions that every group discussed. For each question, ask if any of the groups want to share one or two points that emerged as important for that group. Another way to facilitate a concise report-out is to ask if anything surprising came out of the discussion of that prompt or question. This method avoids long report-out period in which every group lists ideas that other groups already reported. Instead, with a modified report-out technique, you are likely to hear the most important ideas, issues, and concerns from each group. In most cases, once people hear an idea, they know they don't need to repeat it. This makes the report-out faster, more relevant, and dynamic.

KEY TAKEAWAYS

While there are hundreds of facilitation techniques practitioners can select, I have found that the following techniques are among the most effective, while remaining easy and inexpensive to implement. These techniques are effective in a variety of settings, including one-on-one meetings and large public workshops. They can be used for all sorts of activities including visioning, goal setting, brainstorming, evaluating, and prioritizing.

The techniques are:

1. **Productive venting** gives meeting attendees an opportunity to participate the minute they walk into the room (or login to an online meeting). This technique is easy and inexpensive to organize.
2. **Fist to Five** provides a bridge between pure voting and consensus. It is a quick way to gauge the level of agreement in the room while also enabling a nuanced scale of agreement.
3. **Upgraded comment cards** help participants understand what they can influence and where to focus their efforts, bringing new life to an otherwise conventional technique.
4. **Cardstorming/Q-storming** are fun and highly interactive exercises that encourage participation from all types of people.
5. **Small group exercises** help manage large groups of people and bring surprising outcomes, such as improved relationships, increased motivation among participants, and collaborative solutions that go beyond the capacity of any one person.

NOTE

1. Adapted from the International Association of Facilitators description of Fist to Five https://www.iaf-world.org/site/es/articles/2016-07-31/method-month-fist-five

REFERENCES

[1] Sandman, P., *Responding to Community Outrage: Strategies for Effective Risk Communication.* American Industrial Hygiene Association; 1st edition (June 1, 1993), Falls Church, VA. 1993.
[2] Larson, J.R., *In Search of Synergy in Small Group Performance.* 2010, New York: Psychology Press.
[3] Samson, P.L., Fostering Student Engagement: Creative Problem-Solving in Small Group Facilitations. *Collected Essays on Learning and Teaching,* 2015. **8**: p. 153.
[4] Witte, E.H. and J.H. Davis, *Understanding Group Behavior: Volume 1: Consensual Action By Small Groups; Volume 2: Small Group Processes and Interpersonal Relations.* First ed. 2018, Boca Raton, FL: Psychology Press.
[5] Pollock, P.H., K. Hamann, and B.M. Wilson, Learning Through Discussions: Comparing the Benefits of Small-Group and Large-Class Settings. *Journal of Political Science Education,* 2011. **7**(1): pp. 48–64.

Twelve

INTRODUCTION

Despite what many practitioners think, public engagement is not a numbers game. Many of my colleagues recount successful public meetings, surveys, and other activities by telling me the number of people who participated.

We had over 85 people at our public meeting!

We got 3,000 survey responses!

Sure, planners know that it is achievement to get *anyone* to attend a public meeting. And many of us feel it is a big win to persuade even 85 people show up. But as an objective measure, does 85 people equal "success?"

I learned early in my career that even the most straightforward public engagement metrics are subjective and relative. Recently, I worked with a public agency to design and implement a community survey. We distributed the survey online and over the course of six weeks, we received over 1,200 responses. Having developed and distributed dozens of surveys, I knew that most community and neighborhood surveys, regardless of the total population of the municipality, get far fewer responses (usually about 200 to 300 responses). Even though it was an "opt-in" survey, meaning it was not designed to be statistically valid, our team was pleased with 1,200 responses to a survey in a community of 4,000. We proudly announced this number at a subsequent public meeting. But community members at the meeting did not agree with our assessment—and they told us so. Many of them felt a survey response of just over a quarter of the town's population was not enough.

Many local leaders treat public engagement like a numbers game, albeit with relatively small numbers. In an effort to work around subjective metrics (such as the number of people who attend a public meeting), others turn to opinion polling companies for help in designing and distributing community surveys or to find out how community members

DOI: 10.4324/9781003451174-14

perceive a potential decision. Statistically significant surveys are a useful way to ensure that results are representative of a community. Survey results that are statistically significant can more easily be justified in the political sphere. But even the most comprehensive, statistically significant survey has limitations; it does not allow for two-way dialogue or collaborative problem-solving. A survey is a challenging way to generate ideas, promote dialogue, and encourage collaboration. Big numbers, even in relative terms, don't guarantee success.

Given the challenges of measuring success, it may be no surprise that research shows almost two-thirds of planners and decision-makers simply do not try to evaluate their public engagement programs.[1] Many practitioners, wary of attempting to measure their success, ask me questions like the following: *What do we even measure? Do we measure whether everyone was 100 percent happy with the decision? Do we count the number of people who participated? Do we account for whether anyone protested? Or that no one appealed the decision in court?*

The numbers game is an empty promise precisely because it sidesteps the whole point of evaluation in the first place. The purpose of evaluating a public engagement program isn't so we can pad our resumes and collect accolades. The purpose of evaluation is to help us improve our future public engagement programs. Like a decision-making process itself, public engagement cannot be measured solely by the numbers or outcomes. In many cases there are no clear outcomes that can be used to measure the success of public engagement. The good news is that researchers and practitioners in the US and around the world have studied a variety of methods to evaluate public engagement processes with an eye toward helping all of us make constant improvements.[1–8]

A helpful framework for evaluating public engagement includes three types of evaluation criteria: (1) process criteria, (2) outcome criteria, and (3) participant experience criteria.[1] This framework separates the outcomes of a decision from the processes used to engage the public. It further separates the participant experience from the outcomes of a public decision. Using this framework, we can evaluate our public engagement process systematically, but also according to our specific context. Each type of criteria allows a different perspective on what success looks like. This framework helps design an evaluation program that is sensitive to these different perspectives and balances those perspectives with the goals of an organization and the participation objectives set at the beginning of the decision process.

Outcome measures vs. process measures

Outcome measures are what most of us immediately think of when we think about evaluating an experience. When we rate a restaurant, we talk about the food (and sometimes the service). When hospitals measure the success of a health care service, they look at the percentage of patients who died, or the rate of surgical complications. When a company is evaluating its success, it measures the return on investment, which tells them how profitable they are. These are all outcomes. Likewise, we often measure a public engagement process by the end results (or at least what we think the end results are). We count how many people we engaged or how many comments we addressed. We document whether we met the state or federal legal requirements. In some cases, we check the box to state simply whether we engaged the community or not. Outcome measures only tell us about the end results, and only as well as we know what the outcomes are.

While outcome measures can be a useful part of any evaluation process, they also carry limitations. Outcome measures tell us about the results without telling us how that process led to those results. The food we eat at a restaurant represents only the result of a long and complex process. The food on the plate is just one outcome of a process that involves a team of people working together on a long list of complex variables. These variables include where the chef sources her ingredients, the recipes she uses, the methods and skill her staff use to prepare the food, what kind of equipment they use, how they designed the dining room, how they interact with customers, and so forth. Likewise, the mortality rate at a hospital is the result of a multitude of processes, from preventive care to the ratio of providers to patients, to the checklists doctors use when performing procedures.

As we learned in Chapter 8, it is nearly impossible to determine the quality of a decision by its outcome because we would need to be able to measure all the inputs that caused that outcome and we would then need to know all of the outcomes of that decision, even when many outcomes will not be evident until years or decades later. The same can be said of a public engagement process. Measuring the success of that process by its outcomes requires that we know what those outcomes are and that we understand all the externalities that could have caused those outcomes. Just as we do not rate a restaurant based on the process behind the food or measure the hospital by the process they used to save our life, we don't often measure public engagement based on the process we used to get it done.

But measuring the success of a restaurant is very different from measuring the success of a public engagement process. The biggest difference is that restaurants have very clear outcome measures. Does the food taste good? Was it served with a smile? But what is the equivalent in public engagement? At the end of an engagement process, we don't necessarily have a delicious plate of food sitting in front of us. Instead, we have a collection of dozens (and even hundreds) of actions, including people we talked to and perspectives we heard.

Another way to measure public engagement is to use **process measures**. Process measures can be very useful when measuring the success of something as complex as public engagement. Process measures refer to the things we did to complete an engagement program. A process measure tells us if we achieved our objectives in a very simple way: did we do what we said we would do? Instead of measuring the success of a meeting by counting the number of people who showed up, we can ask whether we followed a solid process to design, promote, and facilitate the meeting.

Participant experience measures

While most outcome and process measures can be evaluated by you and your team, the participant experience should always be evaluated by the participants themselves. To do this, we need to ask people for feedback on the public engagement process itself. Some practitioners see this as a form of meta-engagement that only confuses the public. Others are simply afraid to ask. But many practitioners have tracked participant measures to greatly improve their public engagement activities over time.

Participant measures tell us a lot about how the public experiences an engagement activity or program. Were participants comfortable? Motivated? Satisfied? Did they feel listened to? Were meeting times and locations convenient? Naturally, the criteria used to evaluate success of a particular engagement activity will be different depending on the type of activity we are measuring. For instance, we might measure the success of a public workshop differently than a public hearing because those are two different techniques that are designed to meet different objectives. It is important to measure the success of a process based on the objectives for that specific event or process (which you will have defined at the beginning of the decision process).

HOW TO EVALUATE PUBLIC ENGAGEMENT ACTIVITIES

Understanding the level of success in public engagement can best be described as answering the following question: Did we do what we said we would do? In simple terms that means we want to compare the activities we

Table 12.1 Sample Evaluation Measures for Public Engagement

Process Measures

Decisional	*Was the participation process organized around a clearly defined public decision?*
Shared influence	*Was there an opportunity for the public to influence any aspect of the decision?*
Transparency	*Was the entire decision process clearly communicated to the public?*
	Did we acknowledge to the public the challenges we expected to face during the decision-making process?
	Did we communicate the level of public influence over the decision?
	Did we demonstrate that we listened?
	Did we make pertinent information readily accessible?
	Did we explain how public feedback influenced the decision (and how it did not)?
Representation	*Did all affected and interested parties have an opportunity to participate?*
	Did we seek to understand all perspectives and include them in the decision process?
	Did we give special consideration to those who are the most affected but with the least capacity to participate?
Logistics	*Did we initiate public engagement early in the decision-making process?*
	Did we develop a public engagement plan and share it with the public?
	Did we prepare agendas and summaries for all gatherings?

Outcome Measures

Legal outcomes	*Did we follow regulations and meet our legal requirements for public engagement? Was the decision contested or appealed?*
Conflict management	*Did the public engagement process help manage or resolve conflict?*
Legitimacy	*Did the public engagement process generate legitimacy for the decision and the institution/organization?*
Capacity	*Did the public engagement process build institutional and community capacity?*

Participant Measures

Satisfaction	*Did participants report satisfaction and comfort with the process?*

did with our original objectives. For example, if our objective was to provide relevant and timely information about the project, we need to ask ourselves how well we did that throughout the course of the decision-making process. If our objective was to include a wide variety of perspectives from the people most impacted by the decision, we should ask ourselves if we achieved that. Evaluating our public engagement process does not need to be more complicated than comparing what we did to our engagement goals.

Table 12.1 identifies a list of potential evaluation measures that can be easily adapted to fit your specific context. While you and your team can internally evaluate the process and outcome measures by answering the questions, the best way to evaluate participant measures is to ask the participants themselves. This means you will need to create an evaluation form of some sort, whether it is a quick online poll or paper copy of an evaluation form. Appendix A includes a sample evaluation form that can be adapted to measure participant satisfaction.

KEY TAKEAWAYS

1. Evaluation of public engagement is not a numbers game. The purpose of evaluation is to help us improve our future public engagement endeavors.
2. An effective process evaluation uses a combination of process measures, outcome measures, and participant satisfaction measures.
3. Participant measures should be evaluated by the participants themselves.

REFERENCES

[1] Laurian, L. and M.M. Shaw, Evaluation of Public Participation: The Practices of Certified Planners. *Journal of Planning Education and Research*, 2009. **28**(3): pp. 293–309.
[2] Halvorsen, K.E., Assessing the Effects of Public Participation. *Public Administration Review*, 2003. **63**(5): pp. 535–543.
[3] El Ansari, W. and E. Andersson, Beyond Value? Measuring the Costs and Benefits of Public Participation. *Journal of Integrated Care (Brighton, England)*, 2011. **19**(6): pp. 45–57.
[4] Rowe, G. and L.J. Frewer, Public Participation Methods: A Framework for Evaluation. *Science, Technology, & Human Values*, 2000. **25**(1): pp. 3–29.
[5] Uddin, K. and B.M. Alam, *Public Participation Process in Urban Planning: Evaluation Approaches of Fairness and Effectiveness Criteria of Planning Advisory Committees.* Routledge Studies in Urbanism and the City Ser. 2021, London: Routledge, Taylor & Francis Group.
[6] Wang, Z., et al., Construction and Demonstration of the Evaluation System of Public Participation Level in Urban Planning Based on the Participatory Video of 'General Will—Particular Will'. *Sustainability (Basel, Switzerland)*, 2023. **15**(2): p. 1687.
[7] Frewer, L. and A.I.o.F.R.N. Laboratory, *Public Participation Methods: Evolving and Operationalising an Evaluation Framework: Developing and Testing a Toolkit for Evaluating the Success of Public Participation Exercises.* Summary project report. 2001, Norwich: Institute of Food Research.
[8] Mariska Wouters, N.H.-B., and Carla Wilson, Evaluating Public Input in National Park Management Plan Reviews. *Science for Conservation*, 2008. **308**: p. 107.

Thirteen

SOCIAL MEDIA

No one is surprised to hear that a majority of the world uses social media. As of Summer 2023, about 60 percent of the world's population (4.9 billion people) logged into at least one type of social media platform. The average amount of time people spent on social media was about two and a half hours per day.[1] Social media use is much higher among young people, where 84 percent of people 18 to 19 years old use at least one social media platform. More than a third of young people in the US, who are often on the leading edge of social media, use social media "almost constantly" throughout the day.[2] And most people don't just use one platform. It is more common now for social media users to spread their use across multiple platforms, on average, across seven different accounts.[3]

At the same time, political events and cultural expectations have caused the social media landscape to shift dramatically over the last few years, causing millions of Americans to question their personal relationships with these platforms. Perhaps it is a new awareness of the "attention economy" that has led many Americans to reconsider and reduce the amount of time they spend scrolling through social media feeds.[4]

For over a decade, advocates, tech journalists, and policymakers have tracked and communicated the dangers of social media, analyzing how social media impacts the very function (or dysfunction) of our democracy. There is much discussion about how the biggest social media companies have designed algorithms to grab our attention—thereby amplifying conflict, moral outrage, disinformation, and cultivating outgroup animosity. In turn, all of this erodes trust, escalates political polarization, weakens elections, and damages the fabric of our democracy.[5]

The jury is out about whether all of this is a good thing for public health and democracy. A Pew Research Center survey from 2022 concluded

DOI: 10.4324/9781003451174-15

that most people around the globe see social media as "mostly good for democracy."[6] The one exception to that sentiment is among Americans. That same survey of 19 "advanced economies" found that a majority of Americans (64 percent) think social media has been more of a *bad thing* for democracy. Further, 79 percent say social media has made people more divided in their political opinions and 69 percent say it has made people less civil in the way they talk about politics.[6]

In 2023, the US Surgeon General issued an advisory about social media and youth mental health, referencing the growing scientific evidence of "harmful content exposure as well as excessive and problematic use."[7]

Despite the high hopes we had for social media in the 2010s, social media platforms have not grown into the idealized democratic spaces we once envisioned. Another Pew Research Center survey from 2020 of almost a thousand technology innovators developers, researchers, business leaders, and policy leaders found that almost half of those surveyed feared that use of the internet and social media would weaken core aspects of democracy. Key concerns were centered on the role of trust, truth, and democracy. The study concluded, "The misuse of digital technology to manipulate and weaponize facts affects people's trust in institutions and each other. That ebbing of trust affects people's views about whether democratic processes and institutions designed to empower citizens are working."[8]

The criticism of tech companies is focused primarily on how their social media platforms spread misinformation and favor extreme and hateful speech. But there is another issue that should be top of mind for any policymaker involved in public engagement: social media platforms are owned by private, for-profit companies. By design, they are not democratic spaces. Decision-makers at tech companies are not elected by the public, nor are their decisions subject to public scrutiny or involvement. We know that social media companies are structured to maximize profit and accelerate user "engagement" (more on that later), but there is no expectation of transparency when it comes to how the algorithms function or what happens to people's data. There is certainly no expectation that the public should be involved in companies' decisions about how social media platforms are designed whether they align with the public's values.

Social media "engagement" and public engagement

The word "engagement" means a very different thing in the context of social media than it does in the context of public engagement in public decisions. Engagement in social media context is a measure of how much time someone spends viewing or interacting with something in a social media feed; usually that thing is a message that a company, brand, candidate, or influencer wants you to look at. Or it is some other kind of content that is designed to keep you "engaged" with, or otherwise addicted to the platform.

When you read or hear somewhere that social media platforms are "engagement-driven," which doesn't mean the executives working at those companies are seeking feedback from users to help make decisions that impact people's lives. Engagement refers to how much time customers spend using their applications and how often they view, comment, like, share, or somehow interact with the content communicated through their applications. Engagement in the social media context does not refer to a two-way dialogue or a process through which the public can influence decisions that affect their lives. Engagement is about how much time you spend looking at a video or a photo or a message about a product or a brand that is designed to persuade you to do something else, such as buy their product. Because the platforms are optimized to keep users using, they need to constantly push content that will capture our attention. Social media companies have discovered that the best way to capture attention is to elicit extreme emotions, and moral outrage by micro targeting and communicating damaging distortions of reality.

Many of us have heard these criticisms from journalists, advocates, and policymakers: social media captures increasing amounts of our time and attention. Social media platforms tend to favor outrage and hate. And they increase addictive tendencies. I relay this information not for the purpose of attacking social media companies or individuals who use social media. Rather, I share this to help us all consider how planners and local government bodies can and should use social media.

As planners and policymakers, it is our responsibility to consider not only how to use these tools effectively, but also to understand the limits and potential impacts of social media within the larger social context—and especially within the context of modern democracy and local decision-making.

The way you and your organization approach social media may depend on how each of the individuals in your organization view the platforms. Perhaps your team views a lot of the criticisms of social media as unfounded. In that case, your challenge may be a purely practical one; which platforms should you use and how should you optimize staff time and resources to get the most effective results? On the other hand, maybe your colleagues share a belief that social media platforms are inherently corrosive to democracy, even when users have the best of intentions. In that case the issue is more existential; to what extent should you use these platforms at all? And to what extent should you encourage community members to use them?

Like many planners and local government leaders, I view social media platforms as a necessary part of the public engagement landscape. But I also view them with a healthy amount of skepticism about what they can truly offer. There are many existing resources available for planners and local government leaders seeking to build an effective social media strategy. While this book is not intended to provide a point-by-point social media strategy for planners and local governments, I do want to share some key issues and tips that can be helpful when incorporating social media into an overall public engagement strategy.

But first, let's consider some of the ways social media platforms are used, as well as some of the most common challenges faced by local decision-makers.

Popular social media platforms are not optimized for public engagement

Many planners and policymakers view social media as a form of "thin" participation, as described in Chapter 3. Thin forms of participation tend to focus on individual feedback and interactions (such as completing an online survey or petition, stopping by a booth at a festival) and don't require group discussions or a significant time commitment. In that sense, discussion of a public decision on social media may seem like a valuable form of thin participation.

Thin participation may employ online tools that sometimes look and feel like social media. But social media is not necessarily an effective form of thin participation. There are two key distinctions between social media and thin participation techniques: (1) who controls the flow of information and (2) who designs the discussion. Local leaders and decision-makers have little (if any) control over how information flows on social media platforms. And this impairs their ability to create opportunities for open and inclusive discussion.

Social media platforms are not designed to encourage dialogue, thoughtful debate, and problem-solving. That is primarily a function of the prevailing business models, which are designed to extract and sell attention. Personalized news feeds and micro-targeted advertising means that none of us see the same thing when we log in to our favorite platforms. This makes us vulnerable to manipulation while also making it much more difficult to find common ground with our fellow community members. Common ground is the most important component of consensus and compromise.

The conundrum is that while the largest social media platforms are not suited to dialogue and deliberation, they happen to be where many of us find the most people in our communities. So, it is tempting to at least try to leverage these platforms for...*something*.

But it is important to remember that social media platforms are designed with a set of goals that are, in many ways, completely at odds with the goals of public engagement. While there may be ways to leverage these platforms by accessing their ready-made user base, social media platforms are not designed to promote dialogue, collaboration, and group problem-solving.[1]

Social "Listening"

Many state and local government entities have spent over a decade grappling with the challenges of social media, employing a variety of strategies to try to gain control over the various platforms, such as dedicating staff and creating official social media policies. The results of such efforts vary—and many local leaders have turned away from social media altogether due to the challenges of managing information and discussion. Other state and local governments have pursued a different kind of social media strategy entirely: social listening.

Social listening involves analyzing online conversations about a particular topic or brand. A social listening process monitors multiple social media channels, searching for instances when people mention a chosen topic (such as the name of your agency or project), and conducts a sentiment analysis. Social listening can capture what people think about your project and your organization. It can also tell you how people feel about many other topics, what they value, what their goals are, what challenges they face. With the rapid advances in artificial intelligence capacity, social listening tools can and will digest ever larger amounts of information, which ultimately will provide almost instantaneous feedback about what a community is saying.

While social listening can provide valuable insights to local decision-makers, it is important to consider the ethical implications of how this information is ultimately used. Unlike a survey or an opinion poll, people don't necessarily know they are participants in social listening. They didn't necessarily consent. Do planners and policymakers have an obligation to inform people whose sentiments are being scraped from social media platforms and used to help make public decisions? Should the public have a say in which of their sentiments influence a public decision and which do not? The outcome of social listening could mean that members of the public are unknowingly providing feedback, possibly about decisions they know nothing about, and to questions they were never asked.

Is that engagement?

While there is no agreed-upon ethical framework for social listening, some organizations are attempting to establish one. In early 2023, the World Health Organization (WHO) began to explore the ethics of social listening in the public health arena.[9] Social listening in public health is used to gather information about people's health questions and concerns, to understand misinformation about health—and it can be used to help identify outbreaks and behavioral responses. At the same time, WHO acknowledges that collecting and using data presents ethical challenges around privacy, consent, transparency, and accountability. These are many of the same issues faced by planners and local government decision-makers and it will become increasingly important for those of us in the planning and policy profession to be pro-active about the ethical implications of artificial intelligence and the use of social listening outputs.

As planners and local government leaders, we have a responsibility, not just individual users, but as practitioners of democracy, to educate ourselves and cast a critical eye on social media generally, and to understand the larger trends; how do these platforms improve or detract from civil society? How do we make informed decisions about we will use social media in public decision-making processes? Social media platforms can offer some benefits to a well-balanced public engagement program, but they are not optimized for constructive dialogue and public problem-solving.

Leveraging social media in public engagement

Despite my criticisms and caveats, and despite the rapidly changing face of social media, I understand that most public managers are under pressure to leverage social media tools for a variety of reasons. Social media *can* be a helpful supplement to other public engagement techniques but should never be the sole technique used in a public engagement program.

Further, keep in mind that social media platforms are not optimized for dialogue, deliberation, and problem-solving. Given these limitations, below are some of the ways that social media can be used effectively as part of an overall public engagement program.

- **Disseminating information.** Perhaps the most valuable aspect of social media in public engagement is the ability to disseminate information quickly and inexpensively. If your organization or agency has an established social media presence, it can be relatively easy to share information about a project, to redirect users to the organization's project website, to share a link to a survey, or share an invitation to a participation event (such as an in-person or virtual meeting). If your organization does not have a social media presence, you can still disseminate information relatively easily. In this case, find a trusted partner organization that does have a presence and (hopefully) a significant following. Create the content and ask that organization to share it on your behalf. You may lose the ability to moderate any subsequent discussion, so make sure that organization has a strong social media policy and code of conduct that is posted publicly (and hopefully enforced).
- **Live streaming events**. Social media platforms are a convenient place to livestream an engagement event, such as a meeting or workshop (virtual or in-person). Many platforms offer quality accessibility features, such as closed captions and language translation services.
- **Combatting disinformation.** There is at least one major benefit of spending the time and resources to build a presence on at least one of the major platforms and create a strategy to post regular, meaningful content; over time, your organization can develop relationships and credibility, allowing the organization to correct misinformation or disinformation. If disinformation crops up during a specific decision-making process, your agency can leverage its credibility without having to develop a long-standing social media presence on the fly.

Questions to ask when incorporating social media into a public engagement plan

- Does a division or department in your agency already have an established social media presence with a significant following on one of the major social media platforms?

- Does your organization have a strong social media policy and code of conduct?
- Does your agency have staff dedicated to developing and posting original content on a regular basis?
- Do members of the community look to your social media accounts to find information and/or provide feedback about initiatives and decisions?

If you can answer yes to the above questions, it is more likely that you will be able to leverage social media effectively and efficiently.

ONLINE MEETINGS

Online meeting platforms gained a new importance during the COVID-19 pandemic. In early 2020, the primary goal of most online meetings was to ensure the safety of agency staff and the public by allowing people to stay home. The lack of reliable internet access has been considered one major downside of online meetings. But broadband access has become a national priority, and the federal government has invested considerable resources to expand high-speed internet across the US.[10] Despite the downsides, many of my clients and partners discovered a surprising outcome of online meetings: increased participation. Many of my local government colleagues reported to me that more people showed up to online meetings than in-person meetings. They attributed this increase in participation to the following benefits

- Online meetings don't require travel.
- Participants can multi-task while attending an online meeting (such as make dinner, commute on the bus, or drive their kids to soccer practice).
- Online meetings can be recorded and provided on-demand later for people who couldn't attend the live event.

Your ability to use online meeting tools will depend on your community and your agency's technology capabilities, requirements, and budget. That is why I do not explicitly recommend one specific tool or platform over another.

Technical considerations include the overall functionality; how well it integrates with existing technology (such as the agency's website and social media); how easy or hard it is for the practitioner to use; how easily the information can be accessed, exported, and manipulated; level and cost of ongoing support provided by the technology provider; data security; and level of staff training needed to use the tool.

ORGANIZING AND FACILITATING ONLINE MEETINGS

The most important thing to remember when planning an online meeting is that no detail is too small. Online meeting tools offer dozens of features and settings. Each can help or hurt your meeting. Your ability to use these features, and your decision to enable or disable various features, will make all the difference in how successful your meeting is.

Here are the most critical details to get right

- **Learn the lingo.** With online meetings, terms like Host, Panelist, Attendee, Meeting, Webinar, Chat, Backstage, Q&A, and Poll have very specific meanings. It is important to understand and use these terms appropriately when planning your online gathering.
- **Pick the right format for your gathering.** Take special care when selecting your online meeting format. The format is the single biggest determinant of your meeting agenda, including how participants experience your meeting and how much interaction is possible. If you use the most broadly adopted online meeting tools, such as Zoom and Webex, you will likely be choosing between a meeting and a webinar. "Meeting" and "webinar" are not interchangeable terms. They are specific technical terms used by the designers of online meeting platforms, such as Zoom and Webex, to describe features that will determine how your gathering functions. The difference between meeting formats is like night and day and it is imperative to select the right one to meet your objectives. A meeting format allows participants to broadcast themselves on video and to unmute themselves to talk to each other. A webinar does not allow participants to broadcast themselves on video, nor does it allow participants to unmute themselves (only hosts and panelists can unmute attendees). A webinar allows participants to watch a presentation, with few opportunities for interaction. A webinar gives the host more control of what attendees do, but perhaps at the expense of collaboration and discussion. The meeting format allows for large group discussion and small group breakout sessions, but perhaps at the expense of order and control. Another downside of a Webinar is that participants cannot see who else is in attendance, or even how many other attendees are

there. Paradoxically, attendees often tell me they sometimes prefer the highly controlled webinar format (if the Q&A feature is enabled) because they actually worry less that the meeting will veer off the rails. Yet, the number one complaint I hear from attendees about the webinar format is that they can't see who else is there or talk to other participants.

- **Assign a producer.** Don't try to be the host and presenter and run the technical aspects of the meeting at the same time. A producer is a person who oversees making sure the technology works seamlessly, but also does a lot of other things. This person should not have a speaking role in the meeting. This is to ensure that person's attention is focused solely on the technical production. The producer should participate in the meeting as an additional host, giving that person full technical control of all features. The producer will monitor and manage participant arrival, ensure hosts and panelists are visible and audible, assist attendees with technology questions (such as how to turn on a camera or microphone), and manage the Chat and Q&A features if those are enabled. Other issues will invariably come up, such as problems sharing the screen, problems with microphones and the volume of people speaking, echoes, and audio delays. If Q&A is enabled, the producer plays a very important role in managing which questions are answered live, which questions are answered in writing, and which questions are dismissed. Having an assigned producer will ensure that others can focus on hosting and presenting.
- **Do a practice session.** The third most important thing to do when planning an online meeting is to **host a practice session** at least two days before the actual meeting. Online meetings are not like in-person meetings. Online meetings must be carefully choreographed and all hosts and facilitators must communicate how it will run ahead of time. Unlike in-person meetings, it is very difficult to make even the smallest changes to online meetings once they have started. In my experience, the practice run for an online meeting will almost always be messy. But it will allow your team to work out all the technological kinks and issues that you did not anticipate.
- **Double check all settings.** Make sure to use the appropriate settings for "Chat" and "Q&A." Most online meeting platforms allow you to adjust the settings of the Chat so that participants can either communicate with everyone in the meeting, or only with the hosts. These options allow the host to control the amount of chatter happening

while the meeting is ongoing. Know that the Chat will likely be a busy place. Participants will place all kinds of comments in the Chat, including questions about the technology, questions about the meeting format, requests to the hosts, links to websites, words of encouragement, complaints, and comments on the substance of the meeting. While I am an advocate of enabling the Chat, I do not recommend that hosts try to follow along in real time or attempt to use the Chat to record official comments and questions. To set expectations with participants, it is important to communicate explicitly how the Chat will be used and monitored throughout the meeting. If you do not plan to respond to comments or answer questions in the Chat, be sure to remind participants of that multiple times throughout the meeting, as people often drift in and out of the meeting, multi-task while listening to the meeting, or arrive late. Some facilitators ask participants to "sign-in" using the Chat and say something about themselves, which can be a nice way to encourage interaction between community members. But other things can get lost in this exercise. You will need to repeat your instructions for the Chat multiple times throughout the meeting (and preferably present it on a slide). The Chat is a great tool to allow participants in-the-moment opportunities to comment and talk with each other. It is not a good place to store comments for the official record or try to track participant questions. The Q&A feature is a much better place to moderate questions.

- **Learn to use breakout rooms.** People love breakout rooms/groups because they offer an opportunity to talk with other attendees in a more intimate setting than the full group. Breakout rooms are a great place to discuss topics and solve problems.

Though online meetings are effective and beneficial in many ways, planners and policymakers feel the pull to "return to normal," which means go back to hosting in-person meetings like we used to. But for many community members, they can't unsee the benefits of online meetings. They have become accustomed to the ease of attending online, of being able to multi-task during public meetings. They can't or won't take three hours out of their evening to attend an in-person public meeting.

Now that we are a few years removed from the depths of the COVID-19 pandemic lockdowns, many of us face a new push to return to "normal" in-person meetings. This is also combined with the pull of online meetings by a public that has grown accustomed to the convenience. As you can imagine, the conversation within many public agencies leads to one conclusion: let's just do both.

THE DREAM OF HYBRID MEETINGS

At the beginning of the COVID-19 pandemic, my clients and partners expressed excitement about the prospect of someday hosting hybrid online/in-person meetings. The possibility seemed right around the corner. Wouldn't it be cool if we could hold a design charette that would allow someone from Denmark to participate as fully as someone in the room?

In reality, hybrid meetings raised the level of technical complexity of a meeting by a factor of ten. Hosting an in-person meeting that allows full participation by people online turned out to be nowhere near as simple as turning on a camera and plugging the laptop into a loud-speaker. There are dozens of other technological issues and nuances to consider when hosting a truly hybrid meeting.

Conference organizers have figured out how to host effective hybrid events. The cost of those services is unfortunately out of reach for many planners and local decision-makers. I look forward to the day that someone cracks the hybrid meeting to make it simple and affordable for everyday practitioners. For now, I recommend that anyone who wants to host a fully hybrid meeting contract with a specialist and expect to pay more than you would for a regular public meeting.

The pace of improvements in technology means that our ability to host semi-hybrid meetings is also increasing rapidly. Many of us have participated in variations on fully hybrid meetings, such as meetings in which online participants can see a presentation but cannot interact with in-room participants (or vice versa).

For practitioners who would like to conduct semi-hybrid meetings, here are a few practical considerations:

- **Audio.** If you want at-home participants to be able to hear and understand in-person participants, you need to ensure there are microphones around the room and make sure people in the room use them. The most common failure of hybrid meetings is that online participants cannot hear the people in the room and often have no way of communicating that fact to anyone in the room. If you want in-room participants to be able to hear online participants, you need to ensure you have good speakers and a skilled producer to ensure there is no background noise (from online participants who forget to mute) and that there is no feedback from the computer speakers conflicting with the external speakers.

- **Video.** If you want online participants to see what is happening in the room, you will need multiple cameras stationed around the room and the ability to switch between them. Otherwise, online participants will see only the person presenting because that person is usually standing in front of the camera. You can use a second device pointed at the audience in the room. But people at home typically see a tiny square on their screen, meaning that people at home can't really see what is going on in the room, anyway.

- **Organization and staff.** If you want to succeed at a hybrid meeting, you will need additional staff and additional time for organization. You will need more people in the room than a normal public meeting to ensure that technology functions and to facilitate the meeting. You will also need multiple people stationed online to help run the flow of online activity. You may need a person who is stationed in the room and logged into the online meeting to be a go-between. You will need to plan out the logistics of meeting arrival for in-person and online participants, exactly when the meeting will be convened, and who will be the real-time go-between, communicating between the in-person and online participants. Most successful hybrid meetings have a separate facilitator for online participants. While in-person participants have small or large group discussions, the online facilitator will conduct a simultaneous, but separate discussion with online participants only.

Some municipalities have adapted their town board or city council meeting rooms to allow for a simplified form of hybrid meetings. This is feasible because many council chamber rooms were designed to broadcast council meetings on TV. The rooms are set up with a microphone at each councilmember's seat and often with multiple cameras. This set up is more adaptable to hybrid meetings. The downside is that council chambers are not ideal for interactive public meetings, workshops, or small group work.

For communities that don't have the extra budget to purchase high-quality audio/visual equipment or contract with an outside company, my recommendation is to do one or the other; host an exclusively in-person meeting or an exclusively virtual meeting. First host a meeting exclusively in-person. Then replicate that same meeting online, on a different day. If you think this sounds like more work than a hybrid meeting, think again. You could spend the same amount of time and money trying to figure out how to make hybrid meetings work. The replication technique offers another advantage, which is that people who are not available one day, can choose to attend another day.

KEY TAKEAWAYS

1. **The risks of using social media in public engagement.** Key concerns about social media include the harms to mental health and negative impacts on societal trust and democracy. Social media platforms are not optimized for public engagement due to who controls the flow of information and who designs the discussion. Further, the practice of "social listening" (which involves analyzing online conversations about a particular issue or topic) raises ethical questions about privacy, consent, and transparency.
2. **Leveraging social media.** Still, local government organizations can leverage social media platforms by using them to disseminate certain kinds of information, to live stream events, and combat disinformation.
3. **Online meetings** can increase accessibility and overall participation when implemented properly. It is important for local government organizations to learn about online meeting tools (especially the nuances) and practice using them on a regular basis to maintain an understanding of the latest updates and features.

NOTE

1. It is worth noting that a handful of companies have designed effective platforms that *are* capable of promoting dialogue and collaboration, while avoiding some of the pitfalls of the major social media platforms. Examples in 2023 include Social Pinpoint, PublicInput.com, CitizenLab, and MetroQuest. Even though many of these are highly effective tools, their platforms have far fewer regular users (as measured in billions). Using these effective, but lesser-known platforms costs money and requires agencies to build a new audience from scratch by enticing members of the public to sign-up, join, download an app, or create a profile on an unfamiliar website. This so-called "user acquisition" and onboarding can carry significant costs.

REFERENCES

[1] Chaffey, D. *Global Social Media Statistics Research Summary – 2023*. Leeds, UK. 2023.

[2] Emily A. Vogels, R.G.-W.a.N.M., *Teens, Social Media and Technology 2022*. 2022. Pew Research Center, Washington D.C., US.

[3] Wong, B., Top Social Media Statistics and Trends of 2023, in *Forbes Advisor*. 2023.

[4] Odell, J. and R. Gibel, *How to Do Nothing*. 2019, HighBridge: Place of publication not identified.

[5] Rathje, S., J.J. Van Bavel, and S. van der Linden, Out-Group Animosity Drives Engagement on Social Media. *Proceedings of the National Academy of Sciences*, 2021. **118**(26): p. e2024292118.

[6] Pew Research Center, *Social Media Seen as Mostly Good for Democracy Across Many Nations, But U.S. is a Major Outlier*. 2022. Pew Research Center, Washington D.C., US.

[7] United State Surgeon General, Social Media and Youth Mental Health, in *US Surgeon General's Advisory*. 2023.

[8] Pew Research Center, *Many Tech Experts Say Digital Disruption Will Hurt Democracy*. 2020, Washington D.C., US.

[9] World Health Organization, *WHO Kicks Off Deliberations on Ethical Framework and Tools for Social Listening and Infodemic Management*. Geneva, Switzerland. 2023.

[10] Romm, T., Biden Announces $42 Billion to Expand High-Speed Internet Access, in *The Washington Post*. 2023.

Fourteen

How-to materials

Materials in this Appendix:

- Public Meeting Safety Checklist
- Sample Interview Questions for the Engagement Landscape Scan
- Sample Public Meeting Ground Rules
- In-person Meeting and Venue Checklist
- Virtual Meeting Checklist
- Sample Public Engagement Evaluation Form

PUBLIC MEETING SAFETY CHECKLIST

The personal safety of agency staff, facilitators, elected officials, and members of the public is the highest priority at all public meetings, workshops, charettes, hearings, or other public gatherings. To that end, safety should be addressed in all meeting plans and agendas. Create a Public Meeting Safety Plan for all meetings that addresses the following topics:

- **Proper lighting.** Ensure that everyone in the room can see each other, the floors, their seats, and the exits. Don't hold meetings in dark auditoriums. Don't dim the lights for presentations, if possible.
- **Safe seating options.** Ensure that seating options are sturdy enough to hold people and are not prone to collapse.
- **Minimize tripping hazards.** Ensure that there are no power cords crossing the room, boxes or purses placed on the floor, or uneven surfaces that could cause participants to trip and fall.
- **Fire escape routes**. Make sure all fire exits are marked and that any other information about accessing fire escape routes is communicated at the beginning of the meeting. Make sure all facilitators know where to direct people in the event of a fire.

DOI: 10.4324/9781003451174-16

- **Health emergencies.** Have a plan for any unexpected health emergencies. Who on the team is trained in CPR? Who will call 911? Who will close the meeting and manage the crowd during a health emergency?
- **Disruptive/violent participants**

  - Adopt and share a code of conduct/operating values for the meeting.
  - Learn de-escalation techniques for moments when emotions run high.
  - Lead by example by showing respect to all participants.
  - Politely but firmly request that disruptive participants cease the behavior and refer to the code of conduct. Freedom of speech does not protect disruptive behavior. Disruptive behaviors include:

    - Verbally or physically threatening staff, elected officials, or other members of the public.
    - Vilifying someone based on their perceived race, religion, sexual orientation, or gender identity.
    - Shouting or booing from the audience so someone cannot address the group.
    - Refusing to give up the microphone and leave the podium so others can speak.

  - Know what your organization's rights are for removing disruptive, abusive, or violent attendees.
  - Have a plan to adjourn the meeting early if members of the team and the public feel their personal safety is threatened:

    - Store personal belongings of facilitators, staff, and elected officials in a separate room that can be accessed if the meeting needs to be adjourned early.
    - Have a plan for the team to convene in a separate, secure room once the meeting has been adjourned.
    - Have a plan for team members to leave the building safety.
    - Consider ahead of time whether you need to have law enforcement present.

SAMPLE INTERVIEW QUESTIONS FOR THE ENGAGEMENT LANDSCAPE SCAN

In Chapter 9, we learned how to prepare for successful public engagement. After defining a decision and setting objectives, the next step is to conduct a scan of the engagement landscape by asking (and answering) the questions "Who is the public and what do they think?" Chapter 9 describes a process of developing a core participant list and conducting short interviews (20 minutes) with six to eight of these core participants. The purpose of the short interviews is to understand the engagement landscape before finalizing your Public Engagement Plan. Below are sample questions to ask during these interviews. It can be helpful to share these questions with interviewees ahead of time so they can prepare for the interview.

- *To date, what has been your experience with this decision? (i.e. with this problem, issue, initiative, neighborhood, site, corridor, etc.)*
- *How do you think the community will perceive this project/initiative?*
- *What do you think are the community's key concerns about this project/initiative?*
- *What issues or concerns exist around this topic that community members may be reluctant to discuss in a public forum?*
- *What would be the best outcome(s) of this decision?*
- *How would you like to be involved in this decision?*
- *Who else should we talk to at this early stage?*

SAMPLE PUBLIC MEETING GROUND RULES

In Chapter 7, we learned the three key rules of public engagement, which include "Respect the Public." In a public discussion, respect is a collective effort that requires cooperation between the convenors and the participants. To help establish expectations and a common understanding of respectful behavior, it is helpful at the beginning of any public meeting or gathering, to establish ground rules—otherwise known as a code of conduct or operating values. Ground rules can be posted on a slide, written on a flip chart, or printed on a hand-out with copies for everyone. When sharing these with the group, it is important to present them with respect, so that they aren't perceived to be condescending or punitive to participants. In many cases, the ground rules should be written to emphasize the behaviors we *want* to encourage (such as hearing all perspectives) more than behaviors we want to discourage (such as interrupting and talking over others).

Ground Rules:

- Everyone is encouraged to participate
- Respect the agenda and the meeting end time
- Be fully here (or be elsewhere)

- Seek to respect others, even when we disagree
- Attack problems, not people
- Help make sure everyone gets talk time
- Speak from your heart
- Turn cell phones off
- Others? (invite participants to create their own)

IN-PERSON MEETING/VENUE CHECKLIST

The success is in the "little" details

In Chapters 9 and 10, we learned how to prepare for successful engagement, and how to select the right engagement techniques at every stage of the decision. Chapter 11 provided a curated list of techniques that are effective, yet easy and inexpensive to implement in almost any public gathering. Many of the techniques discussed in this book are for in-person gatherings. The success of such gatherings can often come down to logistical details that don't seem important—until the night of the meeting arrives, when they suddenly seem very important.

Below is a checklist of important logistical items to help you pick the right venue and adequately prepare before the night of your meeting. Every item on the list represents something that can significantly impact the comfort of participants and the atmosphere of your meeting. I have personally forgotten to prepare for every single one of these items, at one time or another. This list is meant to help make sure you never do.

- Is the room big enough for your expected crowd?
- Does the venue have chairs and tables that you can move around?
- Are the tables big enough for six to ten people to sit at each?
- Is there good lighting in the room? (Can you find the light switches?)
- Does the venue allow you to provide your own refreshments?
- Is there adequate blank space on the walls to allow you to attach sticky notes or flip chart paper, or affix other kinds of displays if needed?
- Are entrances to the room clearly marked? Can people easily find the room when they enter the building?
- Are there bathrooms? (nearby?)
- Is the space ADA accessible?
- Is there adequate vehicle and bicycle parking?

- Is the venue accessible by transit, bicycle, and walking (if relevant?)
- Is there space in the room to split the crowd into smaller groups?
- Is the available audio-visual technology adequate for your needs—or do you need to provide your own?
- Is Wi-Fi available?
- Will you need a public address system with a microphone and speakers?
- Is there a logical place to set up a camera to livestream the meeting?

VIRTUAL MEETING CHECKLIST

The success is in the teeny, tiny details

Since 2020, about two-thirds of my public meetings are held virtually. Like in-person meetings, the mood and flow of online meetings depends on seemingly minor details.

Below is a checklist of important logistical items to help you set up and facilitate a successful virtual meeting. Every item on the list represents something that can significantly impact the functioning of your meeting.

- Have you selected an online platform that meets your needs?
- Do you understand the difference between a meeting and a webinar?
- Have you reviewed all the settings available to you for your preferred type of meeting/webinar?
- Have you assigned a producer to manage the technical aspects of the meeting and a facilitator to be the emcee and the face of the meeting on camera?
- Have you determined who will fill technical roles, such as Host, Panelists, and Attendees?
- Have you completed a practice session?
- How will you handle the Chat and Q&A features? (will participants be allowed to use those features, and if so, how and for what purpose?)
- How will you accept questions from attendees? (the Raise Hand feature? Q&A feature? Chat box?)
- Do you know who is going to answer questions (either using the Q&A feature or live)?
- Do you have a plan to communicate with your team during the meeting, either via text, a separate online meeting space, or with the backstage function?
- Do you have a plan, in the rare event that the meeting gets hacked

Sample public engagement evaluation form

Please rate your level of agreement/ disagreement with the following statements:	Strongly disagree	Disagree	Neutral	Somewhat agree	Strongly agree
This workshop was a valuable use of my time					
The purpose of the workshop was clear to me					
The meeting organizers explained the public decision we came here to discuss					
I believe that my feedback will influence the final decision					
The time and location of the workshop was convenient for me					
I understand the next steps in the decision process					
The materials presented were clear					
What did you like most about this workshop?					
What did you like least?					
Do you have any other feedback that might help us plan workshops in the future?					

Your name _____. Email _____

Index

Note: Page numbers followed by "n" refer to end notes.

For Product Safety Concerns and Information please contact our EU
representative GPSR@taylorandfrancis.com
Taylor & Francis Verlag GmbH, Kaufingerstraße 24, 80331 München, Germany